The Selective Environment

The Selective Environment

Dean Hawkes, Jane McDonald
and Koen Steemers

SPON PRESS

Taylor & Francis Group

London and New York

First published 2002
by Spon Press
11 New Fetter Lane, London EC4P 4EE

Simultaneously published in the USA and Canada
by Spon Press
29 West 35th Street, New York, NY 10001

Spon Press is an imprint of the Taylor & Francis Group

Typeset in Garamond by M Rules
Printed and bound in Great Britain by
St Edmundsbury Press, Bury St Edmunds, Suffolk

British Library Cataloguing in Publication Data
A catalogue record for this book is available from the British Library

Library of Congress Cataloging in Publication Data
A catalog record for this book has been requested

ISBN 0-419-23530-2

Contents

Preface

> As life has arisen through the hidden aspects of natural laws, so for better or worse the laws of nature command that life make a close adjustment to natural background. The setting is impartial: it can be cruel or kind, but all living creatures must either adapt their physiology, through selection or mutations, or find other defences against the impact of the environment.
>
> (Victor Olgyay, *Design with Climate: Bioclimatic Approach to Architectural Regionalism*, New York, 1963)

This book is about humankind's relation with nature as expressed through the fundamental function of building, of architecture, as a defence against the impact of the environment. Since Victor Olgyay wrote his important book nearly 40 years ago, the tables have been turned. The term 'environmental impact' is now more commonly used to describe the damage that humankind's actions wreak upon nature. The process is now reciprocal. In the past, in seeking to protect ourselves against the rigours of the natural environment, we have slowly, but surely, damaged nature itself. Buildings and the activities performed in them have contributed significantly to this damage.

The aim in writing this book was to show how the buildings that contemporary society inhabits might be brought into a more responsive and responsible relationship with the natural environment. The idea of 'selective' design has its origins in Olgyay's pioneering work and Rayner Banham's seminal account of *The Architecture of the Well-Tempered Environment* (1969). It proposes that the environmental processes of a building should be achieved primarily through its form and construction, and that these should be organised *selectively* to filter the natural environment as the first step in the process of adaptation. The intention is to minimise dependence upon mechanical systems of environmental control and, hence, to limit negative environmental impact.

The preparatory work in the production of the book was

undertaken at the Martin Centre for Architectural and Urban Studies, Department of Architecture, University of Cambridge, with the generous support of a grant from the Mitsubishi Corporation. The authors offer particular thanks to Mr David Pownall for his support throughout the project and at other times. They also thank Eleena Jamil, Welsh School of Architecture, Cardiff University, for her painstaking help in the collation of the illustrations. We would like to thank the relevant individuals and organisations for permission to reproduce the illustrations and have made every effort to contact and acknowledge copyright holders. If any errors have been made we would be happy to correct them at a later printing.

The book is dedicated to Janet Owers, who, in her capacity as Librarian at the Martin Centre, from its foundation in 1967 to her retirement in 2000, contributed so much to the work of the Centre and was of inestimable help to us in this project. We wish her a long and active retirement.

Dean Hawkes, Jane McDonald and Koen Steemers
Cambridge
2001

1　Introduction

The complex art of architecture embraces all of the concerns of the world's cultures. It meets the fundamental need for shelter from the elements, but, almost from its origins, has acquired other purposes and meanings. The Selective Environment is an approach to environmentally responsive architectural design that has developed over a number of years through research which originated in the Department of Architecture at the University of Cambridge. It seeks to make connections between the technical preoccupations of architectural science and the necessity, never more urgent than today, to sustain cultural identity through a time of rapid, global, technological change.

Research towards design

In writing of the development of architectural research at the Cambridge School of Architecture in the 1960s, under the inspiration and direction of Leslie Martin, the architectural critic Robert Maxwell observed that the approach was founded on the belief that research in *architecture* has a separate existence from the associated field of architectural or building science and that, in its fundamentals, the Cambridge approach, as defined by Martin, 'condensed as a love of architecture . . . [that there should be] no artificial opposition between the invention of architectural form and the rational analysis of what had been invented . . . [that] practical reason led on to speculative reason without a break'.[1] In evaluating the environmental strand in the work of the Cambridge school, Maxwell observed that it acknowledged the 'loose fit, that architects know only so well, between form and performance: a space in which cultural pressures can produce strange distortions'.

This book grows out of this tradition of balancing analysis and synthesis in the architectural enterprise and sets out to define a set of simple principles that may guide the design of environmentally responsible buildings appropriate to all cultures and climates.

Architecture and environmental impact

It is now well known that in the countries of the industrialised world, buildings account for a substantial proportion of gross energy consumption. In providing services such as space heating, lighting, ventilation and air-conditioning, buildings may, as is the case in the UK, account for up to 50% of the total energy consumed. As the growing economies of the Third World embrace industrialised technologies, there is a danger that they also will become profligate in their demands for energy.

As a direct consequence of this level of energy demand, buildings have become one of the major sources of environmental pollution. Whether primary fuel is converted into energy via a gas, oil or solid fuel plant within a building, or is converted remotely in electricity generation, it contributes to global levels of environmental pollution.

Buildings and energy demand

The nature of the problem of building energy demand has been recognised since the so-called 'energy crisis' of the 1970s. The connection between buildings and environmental pollution, however, has been acknowledged only in recent years. Consequently, the regulation and practice of building design has changed. In most of the developed world, building regulations concerned with standards of thermal insulation and the efficiency of plants have been improved. In addition, many national and international research and development programmes have led to the development of new components, materials and design concepts for the realisation of low-energy, 'environmentally responsible' buildings.

The result of all of this has been to produce progressive improvements in the performance of buildings. Typically, a conventional building of the 1990s, built to satisfy building

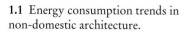

1.1 Energy consumption trends in non-domestic architecture.

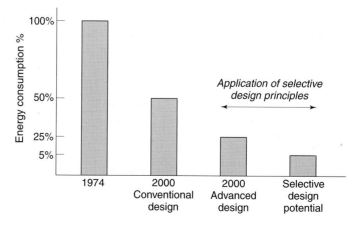

regulations, will consume only 50% of the energy of its equivalent of the 1970s. More advanced designs, which apply more sophisticated design approaches and incorporate improved specifications and materials, can achieve a considerable improvement on this figure. Through these measures, a further 50% saving of energy is quite possible. However, as we move into the new millennium and as the global economy continues to expand, even greater savings will be necessary (Figure 1.1).

To deliver these savings, it is essential that established knowledge should be communicated to general design practice and that the principles developed in the industrialised world be translated into procedures for use in the emerging economies.

The Vitruvian model

Providing shelter from the rigours and unpredictability of the natural environment is one of the most fundamental functions of building. The transition from the unselfconscious building of primitive societies to the self-conscious art of architecture was marked by the codification of the knowledge embodied in vernacular buildings to allow its transmission and application in the design of buildings for many purposes. The earliest surviving account of codified environmental principles in architecture is in Vitruvius's *De architectura*.[2] In Book VI, Vitruvius provided guidelines for the design of houses in the diverse climates embraced by the geographical span of the late Roman Republic. He wrote:

In the north houses should be entirely roofed over and sheltered as much as possible, not in the open, though having a warm exposure. But on the other hand, where the force of the sun is great in the southern countries that suffer from heat, houses must be put more in the open and with a northern or north-eastern exposure. Thus we may amend by art what nature, if left to herself, would mar.

1.2 Vitruvian Tripartite Model of Environment.

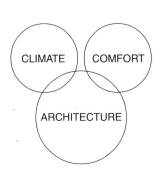

Implicit in this statement, and in much more of the discussion of Book VI, is a simple, lucid model of the environmental function of architecture in which the form and fabric of the building acts to mediate between the naturally occurring environment – *climate* – and the conditions within which human activity may most effectively be conducted – *comfort*. This model, named the 'Vitruvian Tripartite Model of Environment' (Figure 1.2), establishes the principal components of environmental control in all buildings until the development in the eighteenth and nineteenth centuries of new sources of power and the means to harness and deliver them.

The application of 'power-operated' systems in environmental control in buildings was first recorded by Rayner Banham in his seminal work *The Architecture of the Well-Tempered Environment* (1969).[3] There, in his history of environmental design, he defined three distinct 'modes' of environmental control: the 'Conservative', the 'selective' and the 'regenerative'. The regenerative mode is that in which external power is delivered to a building to operate mechanical systems of environmental control. As Banham observed:

it is clear that by the later nineteenth century, the North Americans had acquired habits and skills in the deployment of regenerative environmental aids that were beginning to add up to an alternative tradition.

It was at this moment that buildings became significant consumers of energy and the history of architecture, thereby, entered a new and decisive phase.

Another significant book of the 1960s was Victor Olgyay's *Design with Climate: Bioclimatic Approach to Architectural Regionalism* (1963).[4] In this he acknowledged the significance of the relationship between fabric and plant in modern architecture. Using the terminology of the period, Olgyay offered a model in which the fundamental relationship between 'climatology' and 'biology' was now mediated by the combined processes of 'architecture' and the new component 'technology' (Figure 1.3). By emphasising 'design *with* climate', Olgyay made one of the first significant gestures of resistance to the common assumption in mid-twentieth-century thinking that technology provided the solution to most problems. As an illustration, take Thomas Maver's observation of 1971:

One of the most marked trends in architecture over the centuries has been that of replacing the functions of the building structure by engineering service systems . . . The trend is not likely to be reversed . . . All the evidence points to pressure for greater control in the future.[5]

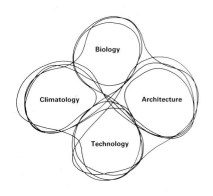

1.3 Model of environmental processes (after Olgyay 1963).

Biology

Climatology

Architecture

Technology

1.4 'Flattening the curve' (after Olgyay 1963).

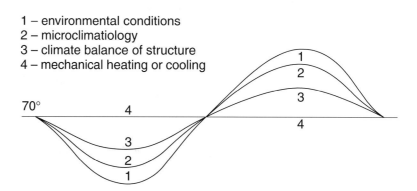

1 – environmental conditions
2 – microclimatiology
3 – climate balance of structure
4 – mechanical heating or cooling

70°

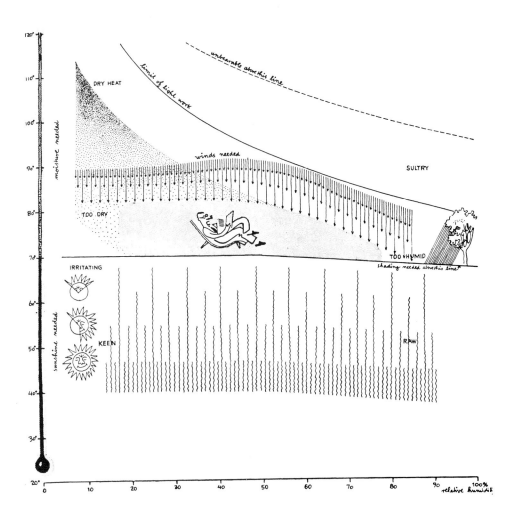

1.5 Bioclimatic Chart (after Olgyay 1963).

But Olgyay, with his 'bioclimatic' approach, argued that the most effective role for mechanical systems is in the final stages of 'fine-tuning' the environmental capability of building structure, not as the primary instrument of mediation. This is elegantly shown in his 'Flattening the curve' (Figure 1.4), which proposes a distinct sequence of actions in proceeding from the varying external environment to the more stable condition of comfort. In his invention of the 'Bioclimatic Chart' (Figure 1.5), Olgyay provided an analytical system by which the relationship between climate and comfort can be clearly established for any given conditions. Then, a simple taxonomy of environmentally determined building types (Figure 1.6) makes it possible to initiate the development of an appropriate design. The idea of 'type' occupies a significant position in the theoretical debate in architecture and, as we will try to show, has particular value in the field of environmental design. In addition, Olgyay – in his wise book – was one of the first to propose the potential of an architecture of *regionalism*, a theme that has since received

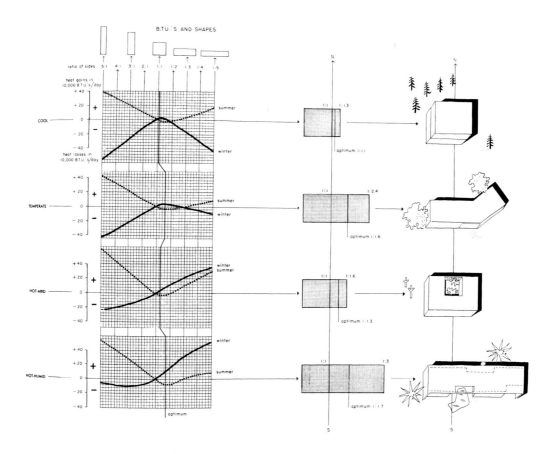

1.6 Taxonomy of environmentally determined building forms (after Olgyay 1963).

much critical attention, particularly in the writings of Kenneth Frampton,[6] and which has much significance in the field of environmental design. This, again, is a matter to which we will return.

Selective environmental design

The principles of 'selective' environmental design have their origins in the work of both Banham and Olgyay. Two important ideas come from Banham. First, the conviction that the problems of the present must be illuminated by a historical sense, that solutions in architecture cannot be fashioned only by the application of pragmatic, analytical processes. Second, the notion of 'modes' of environmental control and, in particular, the term 'selective' itself. From Olgyay, the greatest lesson is the fundamental principle that architecture is at its best when it is working *with* not *against* nature. That the severance of the historical symbiosis with climate was achieved at a cost to both architecture and nature.

In the definition used here, the term 'selective' was first juxtaposed with the alternative, and opposite, category of the 'exclusive' mode of environmental control. This distinction is summarised in Table 1.1. In this definition, the selective mode denoted the possibility of making a return to a rich relationship between climate and comfort in which a building is understood as a complex system of interrelated uses, spaces, materials, components and sources of energy.[7] The approach had the following principal aims:

Aim

- To maximise the use of ambient, renewable sources of energy in place of generated energy.
- To minimise the use of energy-consuming mechanical plant in the processes of environmental control.
- To provide the users of buildings with the maximum opportunity to exercise control over their environment.

Table 1.1
General characteristics of exclusive and selective mode buildings.

Exclusive mode	*Selective mode*
Environment is automatically controlled and is predominantly artificial	Environment is controlled by a combination of automatic and manual means and is a variable mixture of natural and artificial elements
Shape is compact and aims to minimise the interaction between the internal and external environments	Shape is dispersed and aims to maximise the collection of ambient energy
Orientation is relatively unimportant	Orientation is a crucial consideration
Windows are restricted in size and are fixed	Windows are of variable size depending on orientation, room size and function. Solar controls are incorporated on exposed façades
Energy is primarily from generated sources and is used constantly throughout the seasons	Energy is primarily ambient supplemented by generated sources when essential. Use varies from season to season

Climate response

As originally defined, 'selective design' was conceived with reference to the temperate climate of Northern Europe. This, with its relative absence of extremes, but with clear-cut seasonal variations, leads to a 'selective' architecture which expresses, in its form and detail, the environmental differences between northerly and southerly aspects, with plan, form and cross-section being relatively elaborate to maximise the interface between internal and external environments, and with glazing concentrated to the south to exploit useful solar gains to supply space heating in the winter months. From these factors, a distinctive architectural language emerges which is, in some respects, a formal analogue of the conditions of climate in which it is located. This is exemplified in the design of buildings such as the Casa Rurale e Artigianale in Brendola, Northern Italy, by Sergio Los (Figure 1.7) and the Danish architect Erik Sorenson's building for the Cambridge Crystallographic Data Centre in the UK (Figure 1.8). Both buildings demonstrate the importance of the cross-section in environmental architecture. Los's manipulation of the pitched roof form balances the admission of daylight with the control of unwanted solar heat gains in a manner which is in direct lineage from Andrea Palladio's sixteenth-century formulation of exactly the same problem of environmental response to the climate of the Veneto in the *I quattro libri d'architettura* (1570).[8] Sorenson also controls the cross-section of the Cambridge building to limit direct solar gains through the minimally glazed south façade and also to flood the interior with daylight captured by the soaring rooflight. Here, the section also promotes natural ventilation exploiting the stack-effect.[9]

1.7 Casa Rurale e Artiginiale, Brendola, Italy: cross-section. Architect: Sergio Los.

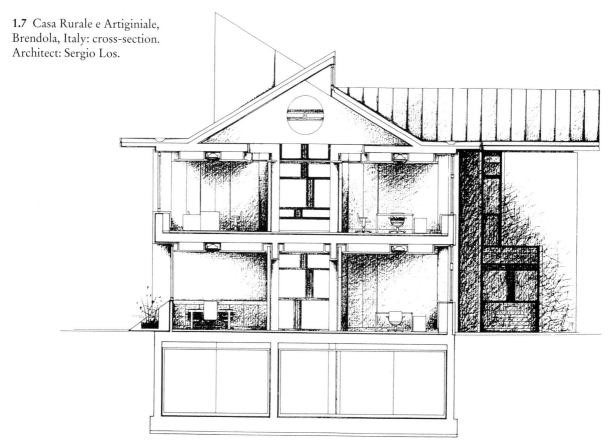

In extending these original principles to the global context, this specific relationship between form and environment must be reconsidered. At the higher latitudes where seasonal variations are marked and the major environmental goal is that of winter heating, the model remains valid, but as latitude reduces and summer temperatures increase, so the environmental priority shifts to address the need for summer cooling. Here account must be taken of the change in solar geometry, with all its consequences for the design and protection of window openings. This is precisely the range and variation of environmental response which Vitruvius described when he set out principles for design in the late Roman Republic, which at that time extended from Egypt to Northern France.

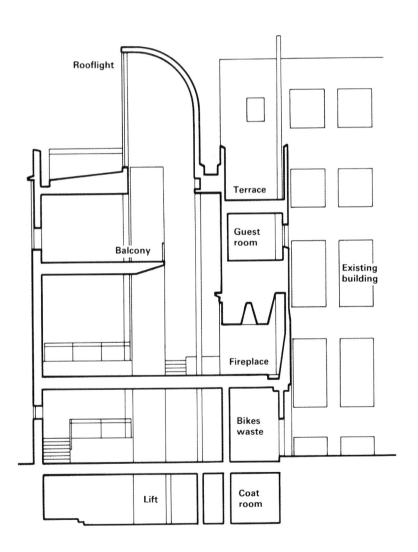

1.8 Cambridge Crystallographic Data Centre, Cambridge, UK: cross-section. Architect: Erik Sorensen.

Moving into the tropical and equatorial regions, where seasonal differences in climate are significantly reduced in comparison with the higher latitudes, the relationship between form and environment is further transformed. A simple comparison between sunpath diagrams and monthly average temperatures in London in the UK and Lagos in Nigeria readily illustrates the point. The shift of the sun from its progress around the southern segment of the sky vault to a high northern latitude in London to its overhead path at the equator at Lagos establishes the essential difference (Figures 1.9 and 1.10). The difference is also reinforced by the contrast in the temperature profiles (Figures 1.11 and 1.12).

1.9 Sunpath diagram for London, UK.

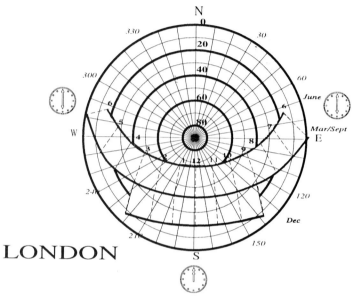

LONDON

1.10 Sunpath diagram for Lagos, Nigeria.

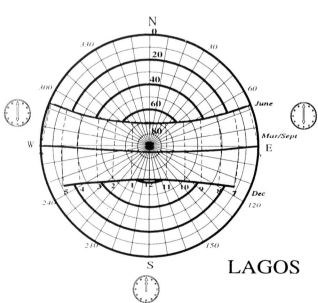

LAGOS

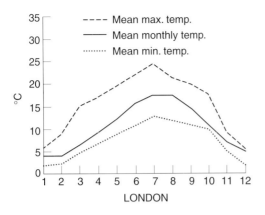

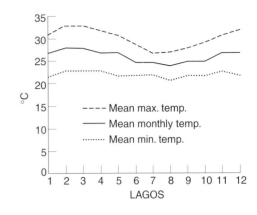

1.11 Monthly mean temperatures for London.
1.12 Monthly mean temperatures for Lagos.

Comfort in the selective environment

One of the central themes in environmental research for much of the twentieth century has been the quantification and codification of the parameters of the thermal, luminous and aural environments. Out of this research have come the precise numerical specifications that form the basis of modern environmental engineering. Indeed, this process was conducted hand-in-hand with the development of electrical and mechanical systems of environmental control and with associated mathematical procedures for their design.

A cornerstone of selective design is the proposition that comfort is a more complex phenomenon than is represented by the familiar and conventional numerical specifications for temperature, ventilation rate, illuminance, and so forth. In the early development of selective theory, an empirical study was carried out on a group of school buildings in the UK.[10]. The study posed four fundamental questions:

- What is the potential for variation of environmental conditions?
- To what extent do the occupants of buildings take active steps to modify their environment, and at what point?
- How wide is the range of environmental conditions tolerated?
- Does this toleration demand changes in activity patterns?

The study showed that the occupants of these buildings placed great emphasis upon their ability to control their environment. It also suggested that comfort has both *spatial* and *temporal* dimensions. In many buildings, the diversity of activity either demands, or may tolerate, variation in the environment from space to space. In addition, there are circumstances in which environmental diversity may occur within a single space and these may contribute to the comfort of the occupants. In this way, a single space may satisfy the differing needs of individuals or, simultaneously, accommodate different activities. Also, in offering control of the environment to the users of buildings, it may be possible for them to achieve a closer fit between activities and environments and, thus, link energy use more closely to human need rather than creating generalised standards of comfort. This may produce valuable savings in energy demand.

A global framework

In its original definition, the characteristics of a 'selective' building were defined by the following parameters:

- internal environment;
- built form;
- orientation;
- fenestration; and
- energy sources.

In adapting the principles to the global context, these may be redefined (Table 1.2). The primary aim remains the same: to seek to achieve the maximum use of ambient energy sources in the creation of internal environments that are, as far as possible, naturally sustained, and in which comfort conditions are related to the climate of the location. It is also assumed that there will be spatial and temporal environmental diversity and that the operation of control systems will be primarily in the hands of the buildings' occupants.

When considering the determination of built form, the question of *shape* becomes more complex. The objective is to maximise the benefits of the ambient environment without suffering unacceptable disadvantages. A key consideration is whether a building has a significant heating requirement or whether it is in a location where cooling is the primary environmental need. This threshold determines whether the form should be developed to admit or exclude solar gains. It also influences the primary decisions about orientation and the detailed design of the fenestration, window size, position, shading and controls.

Many selective buildings will make some use of a mechanical plant in achieving acceptable standards of comfort. However, the relationship between fabric and plant should be approached in a fundamentally different way from that of an 'exclusive mode' design. In traditional buildings in temperate climates, the heating system, whether an open fire or central heating installation, was seen as an adjunct to the environmental control provided by the fabric. It was used only when the fabric alone failed to provide

Table 1.2
Global characteristics of selective design.

Internal environment	Standards are related to the local climate. Emphasis is on the maximisation of natural light. Primary temperature control is by the building fabric. There is spatial and temporal diversity of conditions. Control is by the occupant
Built form	Related to the specific climate. Cross-section is a key element of the environmental response
Orientation	Related to the specific climate. There is reference to a sunpath diagram
Fenestration	Related to the specific climate. The window area should balance the relationship between the thermal and luminous environments in relation to local climate
Energy sources	Should be primarily from ambient sources: natural lighting, exploiting passive solar gains and natural ventilation where appropriate. Mechanical systems for heating, cooling, ventilation and lighting should be regarded as supplementary to the primary control provided by the 'selective' built form. Direct use of renewable energy sources through photovoltaic and water-heating systems should be considered

acceptable conditions. One of the fundamental conceptual shifts in the development of the exclusive mode was the assumption that the plant was a *primary* agent of control. In selective design, auxiliary systems should be regarded as *secondary* to the environmental function of the fabric. Their function is to 'fine-tune' the environment within the parameters defined by the design of the envelope. This principle applies to all mechanical plants: heating, cooling, ventilating and artificial lighting. Just as in conventional heating system design, where the concept of the 'heating season' is applied, so there should be a 'cooling season', a 'ventilating season' and a 'lighting season'.

Procedures for selective design

In beginning the design of a selective building, the first step is to construct a description of the climate at its location. In all cases, the principal parameters of climate are temperature and solar geometry. From examination of temperature data, the need for a strategy for heating, cooling or both will be established. This will direct the development of the design towards means of *collecting* or *excluding* solar radiation and indicate the degree to which the construction will need to provide thermal insulation, to control the flow of heat through the envelope, and of thermal mass to moderate the impact of heat gains upon the internal temperature. Data on solar geometry provide the basis for the development of built forms that admit or exclude solar radiation. They also inform the design of fenestration and shading systems.

Chapters 6–8 will illustrate, through both theoretical and practical cases, the translation of *principle* into *form* in selective design.

References

1   Robert Maxwell, 'Foreword', in Dean Hawkes, *The Environmental Tradition: Studies in the Architecture of Environment*, E & FN Spon, London, 1996, pp. 6–8.

2   Marcus Vitruvius Pollio, *De architectura* (1st century BC); English trans. Morris H. Morgan, *Ten Books on Architecture* [1914], Dover, New York, 1960.

3   Rayner Banham, *The Architecture of the Well-Tempered Environment*, Architectural Press, London, 1969.

4   Victor Olgyay, *Design with Climate: Bioclimatic Approach to Architectural Regionalism*, Princeton University Press, Princeton, 1963.

5   Thomas Maver, *Building Services Design: A Systemic Approach*, RIBA, London, 1971.

6   Kenneth Frampton, 'Towards a critical regionalism: six points for an architecture of resistance', in Hal Foster (ed.), *Postmodern Culture*, Pluto, London and Concord, MA, 1983.

7   Dean Hawkes and Hayden Willey, 'User response in the environmental control system', *Transactions of the Martin Centre for Architectural and Urban Studies*, 2, 1977.

8   Andrea Palladio, *I quattro libri dell'architettura*, Venice, 1570; English trans. Isaac Ware, *The Four Books of Andrea Palladio's Architecture*, London, 1738; repr. *Andrea Palladio: The Four Books of Architecture*, Introduction by A. K. Placzek, Dover, New York, 1965.

9   For a detailed description of these buildings, see Hawkes, *The Environmental Tradition*.

10 Diane Haigh, 'User response in environmental control', in Dean Hawkes and Janet Owers (eds), *The Architecture of Energy*, Construction Press/Longman, Harlow, 1982.

2

Nature, architecture and environmental inquiry

The relationship between architecture and nature has long been the subject of critical attention. Now, fuelled by popular concerns about the future sustainability of the planet, the relationship has been given fresh emphasis as the new scientific and technological advances associated with energy conservation are applied to the design of buildings.

Projection of human need: sanity and nature

The desire to maintain close contact with nature to maintain human dignity and morality is a common theme in Western art and literature. Polite society has often appropriated rural ideals in the representation of its fascination with nature. The neo-pastoral romance of the seventeenth and eighteenth centuries was frequently expressed through the medium of architecture. Implicit in this was a sense of the relationship between human well-being and contact with nature.

In *The Country and the City* (1973), the cultural commentator Raymond Williams described a new consciousness of nature that emerged with the Industrial Revolution:

There is the separation of possession: the control of land and its prospects. But there is also a separation of spirit: a recognition of forces of which we are part but which we may always forget, and which we must learn from, not seek to control. In these two kinds of separation the idea of Nature was held and transformed.[1]

There are many precedents for studies of nature and climate in architecture. One of the most frequent references in the literature of environmental design is to primitive architecture. Joseph Rykwert's *On Adam's House in Paradise* (1972) suggested that this reveals a need to return to a state of being that has not been 'degraded' by cultural symbolism. He argued that it indicated the realignment of purpose and of taking stock:

The return to origins always implies a rethinking of what you do customarily, an attempt to renew the validity of your everyday actions, or simply a recall of the natural (or even divine) sanction for your repeating them for a season.[2]

This development of a theoretical ground that keeps faith with the forces of nature has deep social and cultural roots. However, primitive architecture is a common source of interest for environmental enquiry, and not only because it is perceived as being uncorrupted by self-conscious taste and fashion. Traditional settlements and their vernacular architecture often demonstrate adaptations to natural forces that have an authority analogous to that of biological natural selection. The settlements show how humankind has utilised available resources in the quest to establish some stability in the face of the uncontrollable variations of nature.

Such studies form a significant body of knowledge from which the relationship between climate and architecture may be understood. Their use as a reference for contemporary design, however, has obvious limitations because of the vastly different cultural, functional and technological demands made of buildings in the twenty-first century. The theme of the value of tradition and use of the vernacular is of great interest when one considers the nature of an appropriate architecture for the emerging economies.

'Nature is firing back'

The title of this section comes from Mete H. Turan's *Design for Arid Regions*. It is used to symbolise the shift in the valuation of nature that has followed from the growing awareness of the damage that human activity has done to the environment. The strategy of interpreting climatic settings for architecture is complex, as the following chapters will show. Now the impetus for perfecting our interpretation is new and urgent.

Some believe that this shift of ground is a function of much more than the so-called 'energy crisis'; more than the conservation of finite global resources; more than the maintenance of our present standards of comfort for the consumption of less energy; or of the idea of sustainable energy supplies. It may be interpreted as a necessity for the intellectual and moral survival of humankind, a response to the dislocation from natural forces created by the impact of technological change and the economics of consumerism.

Turan, drawing on references to the social theorists Manheim, Leiss, Joseph Engels and Marcuse, contended that the environmental praxis of vernacular architecture was the result of the dialectical dialogue between man and nature. This continuity, he argued, enabled the cultural symbolism of architecture to be preserved and developed, but that now we have lost our environmental consciousness and that nature is 'firing back at its masters'. Turan wrote:

The environmental conditions we confront today are fundamentally the result of the idea of an external nature outside of man and the vulgar pragmatic conceptions of mastery over nature ... Therefore, modern scientific rationality ruled by pragmatism and instrumentalism is far from bringing alternative solutions to the technological problem of mastery over nature.[3]

Under the impact of technological change, there is a growing consensus that architectural objectives and procedures should be realigned to reflect our improved climatic awareness. Global climate change is an issue of widespread social and political concern as is witnessed by international accords such as the Montreal Protocol of 1989, under which the US government called for a stop to the production of chlorofluorocarbons (CFCs) by 1996, the Earth Summit of 1992, held in Rio de Janeiro, at which limits to the emission of carbon dioxide gas (CO_2) were agreed by the major industrial nations, and the subsequent determination of the 1998 Kyoto Summit.

The environmental impact of buildings is widely acknowledged and, in the past quarter-century, much progress has been made in developing the means to reduce it through technological development and scientific analysis. However, there is a need to locate these within comprehensive architectural paradigms that connect them to the wider, historical, cultural and social discourse, without which technology remains of purely instrumental value. The Selective Environment is a response to just this challenge.

Literature of environmental design: interpretation and practice

If you merely read this book you will not reach the way of strategy. Absorb the things written in this book. Do not just read, memorise or imitate, but so that you realise the principle from within your own heart study hard to absorb these things into your body.[4]

One consequence of our contemporary concern with questions of energy and environment in building design has been an explosion in the literature for design guidance. Much of this presents the results of research conducted in 25 years since the 'energy crisis' of the early 1970s and, in its sheer quantity, is almost certainly the largest body of technical information on a single topic ever produced for building designers.

In principle, it is entirely proper that the results of fundamental research should be published objectively and that their adoption and interpretation be the responsibility of those who choose to apply them in practice. One of the difficulties in designing energy-efficient, environmentally responsible buildings is that the process entails the orchestration of many parameters drawn from several disciplines. Without an overall 'conceptual model' to define fundamental relationships between the parts of the problem, there is a danger that the results of research will be misinterpreted or disregarded. There is a need, therefore, to construct broad frameworks within which specific procedures and data may be applied, and which connect the predominantly technical concerns of energy and environmental research to the contextual and programmatic circumstances to which all building design must respond. This problem of achieving a judicious balance between speculums and generalisation is central to architectural design.

It is this book's intention to propose just such a framework. By reference to the 'Vitruvian' model described in Chapter 1, we see the problem as achieving the transformation of the uncontrollable, widely variable external climate into a more narrowly defined and controlled set of conditions in which human activity may comfortably take place. The agent for this transformation is the building and the priority is to achieve the maximum degree of control through the medium of the building fabric. Mechanical systems, if they are to be used, are applied to the 'fine-tuning' of the internal environment at those times when the unaided fabric fails to do the job.

To realise this objective, precise formulations or prescriptions have been deliberately avoided. In the following chapters, Chapter 3 discusses the wide socio-political background to the global environmental picture through a comparison of the 'climates' of Europe and Africa. We then move on to a consideration of the two poles of the 'Vitruvian' model – the *given* of climate and the *goal* of comfort. Again, the approach is indicative and discursive rather than precise and prescriptive.

One of the most difficult steps in the design of a building is to translate a statement of the problem into a convincing solution. It is particularly difficult to bridge the gap between the abstractions of the analytical procedure of building science and the concrete necessities of architectural form. We try to solve this problem in three ways. First, a group of 'generic studies' is presented in which the connection between climate and form is made explicit for the contrasted conditions of London and Lagos. Whilst these studies themselves only represent primitive approximations to the complexity of real buildings, their very simplicity allows complex relationships to be made explicit. The argument for this kind of study is presented at some length as a prelude to the data themselves. Second, a selection of 'case studies' of designs is presented that demonstrates how the principles of the 'selective environment' may be translated into specific solutions for buildings of many types for locations around the world. Third, the tool used to connect theory to practice is the 'checklist'. This familiar device is used here to draw attention to the principal factors that a designer should take into account in the development of a 'selective' building. The checklist is structured sequentially, proceeding from the large to the small scale and from the architectural to the mechanical.

References

1 Raymond Williams, *The Country and the City*, Chatto & Windus, London, 1973.

2 Joseph Rykwert, *On Adam's House in Paradise*, Museum of Modern Art, New York, 1972.

3 Mete H. Turan (ed. Gideon S. Delaney), *Design for Arid Regions*, Van Nostrand Reinhold, New York and London, 1983.

4 Miyamo Musashi, *Go Rin No Sho*, 1645; English trans. Victor Harris, *A Book of Five Rings*, Allison & Busby, London, 1982.

3 Context: the regional dimension

The fundamental strategy of Critical Regionalism is to mediate the impact of universal civilisation with elements derived indirectly from the peculiarities of a particular place ... The case can be made that Critical Regionalism as a cultural strategy is as much a bearer of world culture as it is a vehicle of universal civilisation.[1]

In his advocacy of 'Critical Regionalism' as a strategy for architectural design, Kenneth Frampton drew attention to the tension that exists between the global concepts and technologies which have played such a fundamental role in defining the architecture of the twentieth century and the value which we continue to place upon the expression of the web of circumstances that distinguishes one place from another. The argument is complex and wide ranging, but one passage in Frampton's chapter, in the section called 'Culture versus nature', directly addresses the question of the relationship between climate and architectural form.

Discussing 'the contingencies of climate and the temporally inflected qualities of local light', Frampton wrote:

the sensitive modulation and incorporation of such factors must almost by definition be fundamentally opposed to the optimum use of universal technique. The generic window is obviously the most delicate point at which these two natural forces impinge upon the outer membrane of the building, fenestration having an innate capacity to inscribe architecture with the character of a region and hence to express the place in which the work is situated.

A constant 'regional inflection' of the form arises directly from the fact that in certain climates the glazed aperture is advanced, while in others it is recessed behind the masonry façade.

The way in which such openings provide for appropriate ventilation also constitutes an unsentimental element reflecting the nature of local culture ... the main antagonist of rooted culture is the ubiquitous air-conditioner ... Wherever they occur, the fixed window and the air-conditioner are mutually indicative of domination by universal technique.

This 'unsentimental' view of climatic regionalism has distinguished antecedents in the literature of architecture. It is not too far-fetched to cast Vitruvius's *De architectura*, with, as noted above, its careful prescriptions for design in response to the enormous climate range of the late Roman Republic, as a regionalist text. More recently, as seen in Chapter 1, Victor Olgyay's *Design with Climate: Bioclimatic Approach to Architectural Regionalism* (1963) applied systematic analysis to demonstrate explicitly the relation of climate and form. *The Selective Environment* is an attempt to extend that tradition.

It is impossible to describe the complex, cultural, social and technological phenomenon of architecture without reference to its history. The survival of buildings from the past and the vast body of literature on the history of architecture is, in effect, what defines the discipline as it is generally understood and taught in schools of architecture, and which implicitly underlies the best architectural practice. On the other hand, the *geography* of architecture receives relatively little attention. In *The Englishness of English Art* (1965), Nikolaus Pevsner superimposed a specific geographical framework upon what was, in reality, a work of art history and, in so doing, illustrated some recurrent characteristics of English art and architecture.[2] However, before the question of regionalism attracted attention in the 1980s, geography, in its global dimension, played relatively little part in the architectural discourse. As practice becomes increasingly international and architects work in places far from their native environments, it becomes essential for geography, or, to be more precise, those parameters of design which are geographically determined, to be understood more than ever before.

One of the most clear-cut ways in which the relationship between climate and building may be revealed is to look at vernacular buildings. As Amos Rapoport has shown in his influential *House Form and Culture* (1969), vernacular buildings may be interpreted in some cases as an almost direct analogue of the climate of the place in which they are built.[3] Questions of form – whether compact or dispersed, of orientation – whether to admit or exclude the sun, of the size and disposition of openings, of the design of shading devices, of whether to adopt massive or lightweight construction, and so on, are frequently eloquently illuminated by studies of the vernacular. However, the different scale, function and technology of modern practice inevitably limits the direct value of these studies.

When one considers the global context within which architecture functions in the modern world, other geographically founded factors must be noted. To establish the essentials of the selective strategy, a comparison will be drawn between the warm temperate climate of Europe and the hot humid conditions of equatorial Africa. In addition to outlining the dramatic physical contrast between these locations, the comparison also reveals vital socio-cultural differences which, ultimately, bear profoundly upon architectural design.

An average American or North European consumes ten to fifteen times as much primary energy to sustain their lifestyle as the average African. There are regions of the USA and Africa whose climates, described by the conventional physical parameters, are virtually identical, but the assumptions about the precise nature of an appropriate architectural response may, of necessity, be very different.

Climate of interest

In the UK, over the last 20 years, the annual consumption of primary energy has been relatively constant, but that energy has been utilised with greater efficiency. Improvements in standards of thermal insulation, which are demanded in new buildings by Building Regulations, and progressive improvement of the fabric and equipment in the existing building stock have been successful in containing the environmental impact of the continuing development of the built environment. This should not be ground for complacency, however, since buildings, as is frequently observed, account for over 50% of the primary energy consumed in the developed world. However, the situation in underdeveloped and developing countries is quite different. As these societies strive to make economic progress, they become locked into a rerun of the equation of economic growth with energy consumption that characterised the first Industrial Revolution.

The levels and patterns of urbanisation in Africa contrast strongly with those in Europe. The continent of Africa has an overall density of nine persons per square kilometre compared with 85 persons in Europe. There is, however, a strong historical connection between Europe and Africa wrought through the legacy of colonialism. Many African cities reveal the effects of this legacy in their urban structure, institutions and built form. Pre-colonial Africa had few towns; most modern African cities were established by Europeans as centres of colonial administration.[4] East Africa had the lowest level of urbanisation and Central African towns were almost all of European origin. West Africa had a long history of urbanisation that had produced clusters of urban development.

In modern times, the rate of urbanisation increased in the 1950s, but in the 1960s Africa still had a low level of urbanisation.

Less than 10% of the population lived in cities and there were only three cities with over 500,000 inhabitants and none of over 1 million. Between 1960 and 1980, however, there was a rapid growth in the rate of urbanisation. A mass exodus of people from rural areas led to the growth of extensive shantytowns around the major locations of economic activity. A 'primate city' is defined as one that is more than twice the size of the next largest. In many countries this is the capital, and it was these cities that experienced the most rapid growth. The trend has continued and there is the prospect that a continent that within living memory had a rural economy will become predominantly urban early in this century.[5]

Paradoxically, the form and social structure of the African city continues to be seen as a direct consequence of colonial exploitation. There is a view that colonialism created an 'ecological segregation' that has inhibited the mature development of an African city and which reflects the specific social and economic circumstances of that continent:

Population, economic activity and with them wealth and power are becoming increasingly concentrated in ever more restricted portions of the national space economy, thus intensifying imbalances and widening the gap between richer and poorer. Depending upon one's viewpoint, either the urban system is working weakly as a channel for innovation diffusion with limited trickle-down and spread effects, or the exploitative role of the urban system with the 'head link' city at its pinnacle, is progressively under developing the area with which it is in contact as surplus profit is directed by way of the centres in the system into the core region of the world economy.[6]

The future pattern of development in Africa has been the subject of numerous economic theories and speculations. Some examples are listed here:

- The establishment of 'growth centres' that contain a series of industrial enterprises to stimulate the emergence of specialised services.
- The stimulation of the rural economy as a means of slowing down the rate of urban growth.
- Capital relocation, such as from Lagos to Abuja in Nigeria.
- The development of secondary cities in an attempt to create intermediate economic development areas.

Over-rapid urbanisation associated with neglect of rural areas and more particularly of agriculture and soaring staple food imports is the most serious problem facing tropical African states in the closing decade of the twentieth century.[7]

It is essential that Africa and other developing regions should construct their own environmental agenda if they are to avoid the re-enactment of the environmental history of the developed world. Pascal Gayama, of the Organisation for African Unity, reinforces this view:

Africa has been involved in setting the new world environmental order through its involvement in the 1992 UN Conference on Environment and Development (UNCED) in Rio de Janeiro. Africa went into the negotiations with its own agenda and priorities. The fact that some of Africa's concerns were not taken into consideration in Rio does not mean that Africa will not protect its own environment.[8]

Indigenous is not necessarily vernacular

The relationship between vernacular building and the design of appropriate buildings to house contemporary needs is not simple. It is tempting to imagine that structures that have evolved through a kind of *architectural Darwinism* of trial-and-error over many years, perhaps centuries, will contain an embodied wisdom that lies latent, awaiting rediscovery. This may sometimes be the case, but there are many reasons why great caution must be exercised before placing too much reliance on these models.

Studies such as Rapoport's *House Form and Culture* and the parallel and more specifically located work of Susan Denyer's *African Traditional Architecture: An Historical and Geographical Perspective* (1978)[9] show how indigenous structures embody complex interactions between physical and cultural factors. These can easily conceal the actual relationship between building form and its climatic context by the elaboration of the 'primitive' form which for cultural reasons has come to carry overriding priority. In some cultures, the *techno-centric* preoccupations of industrialised societies may be profoundly irrelevant. In other circumstances, the limitations of the available materials may demand a solution that, whilst best in the circumstances, may fall well short of the ideal that easily available modern materials can achieve.

In Africa, the geographical scale, climate variation and cultural complexity makes it impossible to derive a clear-cut paradigm for new building from the indigenous building culture.[10] On the other hand, there is a need there, and in other emerging economies, to resist the lure of the new global 'vernacular' of the glass-walled, high-rise, air-conditioned building. Wherever it is found, and whether it houses a corporate headquarters, an international hotel or a university, this type of building represents an attitude of technological confrontation with its environment

3.1 Elizabethan house at Great Waltham, Essex, UK.

which is an affront to our new-found environmental sensibilities and obligations. Even in its 'homeland' of North America and Europe, it now 'enjoys' a problematic reputation, which renders its relevance to other contexts even more dubious.

The similarity of the central business districts all over the world illustrates the success of the technologically based modern skyscraper in becoming the icon of global capitalism. On the other hand, the contrast between indigenous buildings from different climates, such as between the UK and Nigeria, suggests something of the cultural poverty of the skyscraper in those climates (see Figures 3.1 and 3.2). The juxtaposition of *international civilisation* and *regional cultures* could not be more convincingly demonstrated.

The task for contemporary 'unsentimental' environmental regionalism is to discover a way of translating the objectivity of architectural science into designs for buildings that meet the needs and aspirations of the sophisticated, diverse and rapidly evolving cultures that now populate the planet. There is a pressing need to articulate general principles from which designs may be developed and, as a vital part of this process, to find ways by which the abstract formulations of architectural science may be translated into concrete paradigms for architectural form.

3.2 African house: cross-section
(after Denyer 1978).

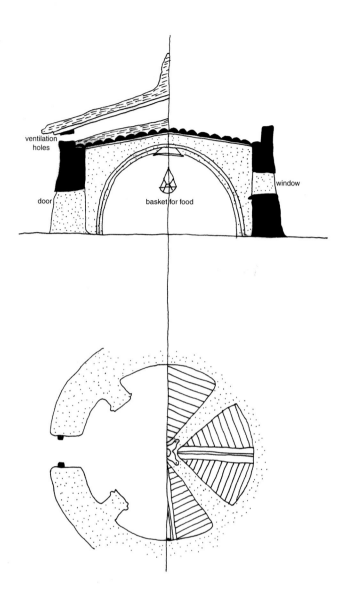

References

1 Kenneth Frampton, 'Towards a critical regionalism: six points for an architecture of resistance', in Hal Foster (ed.), *Postmodern Culture*, Pluto, London and Concord, MA, 1983.

2 Nikolaus Pevsner, *The Englishness of English Art*, Pelican, Harmondsworth, 1965.

3 Amos Rapoport, *House Form and Culture*, Prentice-Hall, Englewood Cliffs, NJ, 1969.

4 The East African Royal Commission noted in its Report (1955) that the growth of towns was the result of non-African enterprise.

5 Thomas L. Blair, 'Shelter in urbanising and industrialising Africa', in Paul Oliver (ed.), *Shelter in Africa*, Barrie & Jenkins, London, 1971.

6 Abedayo Adeji, *Africa Within the World*, African Centre for Development and Strategic Studies/Zed, 1993.

7 M. B. Gleave, 'Urbanisation', in *Tropical African Development*, Longman, Harlow, 1992.

8 Pascal Gayama, 'Africa's marginalisation: a perception not a process', in Adeji, *Africa Within the World*.

10 Susan Denyer, *African Traditional Architecture: An Historical and Geographical Perspective*, Heinemann, London, 1978.

4 Comfort and climate in the selective environment

As life has arisen through the hidden aspects of natural laws, so for better or worse the rules of nature command that life make a close adjustment to natural background. The setting is impartial; it can be cruel or kind, but all living species must either adapt their physiology through selection or mutations, or find other defences against the impact of the environment.[1]

The 'Vitruvian' model of environmental control indicates the function of architecture in transforming the conditions of the naturally occurring climate into the more constrained set of conditions to which we conventionally ascribe the notion of comfort. Most human activities benefit from protection from the wind and rain and some limitation of the range of variation in the thermal, visual and aural environments.

Building science and comfort

One of the central themes of modern building science has been to establish an objective understanding of the relationships that exist between the environmental conditions which may be created within buildings and human responses to these conditions. R. G. Hopkinson, one of the greatest building scientists, made a simple but fundamental distinction between two kinds of 'stimulus–response' relationship, which he labelled the 'linked' and 'unlinked' relationships (Figure 4.1).[2] These demonstrate how, sometimes, the more we have of a particular element of the physical environment the better we like it – as generally applies in the case of light, where *visual acuity* improves as illuminance increases. On the other hand, there are familiar cases where the more we have, the less we like it – as is the case with noise. These are the *linked* relationships. However, if we consider the way in which we respond to the stimulus of heat, for example, the relationship is more complex. We are uncomfortable when there is too little heat, when we are *cold*, and also uncomfortable when there is too much heat, when we are *hot*. Thermally, we are comfortable at some intermediate point, when neither cold nor hot. Even in the linked situations, the relationship is not as simple as it may first seem. For example, the effect of high levels of illuminance can often lead to the experience of *glare*, when some brightly lit places become uncomfortable. A possibly even more complex situation may occur when we positively seek an environment that orthodox theory would suggest should be uncomfortable. An example is the pleasure derived from very loud music in discotheques or concert halls and the effects of stroboscopic lighting which accompany music in nightclubs, although seldom in the concert hall.

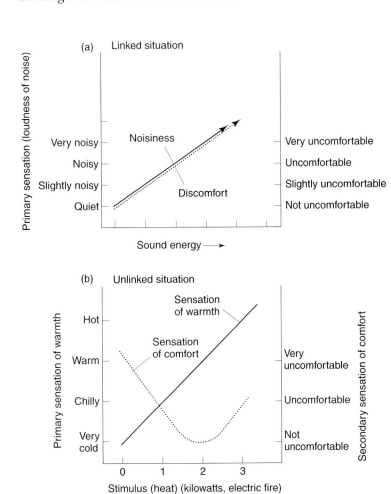

4.1 Relationship between stimulus and response: (a) 'linked' and (b) 'unlinked' situations (after Hopkinson 1964).

The observable relationships between a property that may be observed, and measured and predicted, about the desired environment within a building and the conditions that support human activity underlie the codified environmental standards which are the basis of modern environmental design practice.

The design manuals contain tables of recommendations for temperatures, light levels and noise levels deemed desirable for the performance of an enormous range of activities. These constitute a base from which sound practice may begin, but much recent research has demonstrated that the nature of comfort is more complex than is implied by these simple prescriptions.

Taking the case of thermal comfort, it can be shown that the interaction between the human body and the environment in a building is more than a matter of specifying air temperature. Olgyay showed that the thermal environment is made up of radiant, conduction and convection components that impinge on the body in various, and often varying, combinations (Figure 4.2). In almost any practical environment there will be a complex mix of air temperature, radiant temperatures – some high, some low – and patterns of air movement, which are the actual determinants of comfort.

4.2 Man–environment relations (after Olgyay 1963).

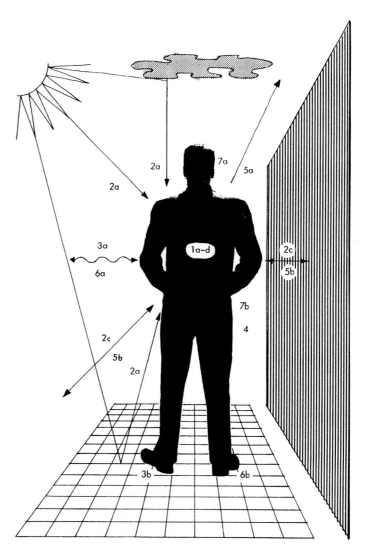

One of the most important comfort research studies of recent years was undertaken by Michael Humphreys at the Building Research Establishment in the UK.[3] In this he correlated reported internal temperatures with measures of the ambient temperatures in places distributed over much of the globe. This showed very clearly that thermal comfort is not a matter of simple physiology, in which 'optimum' conditions may be universally proposed. The findings confirmed the 'common-sense' perception that people who live in hot places are comfortable at higher temperatures than those in cooler regions. But its finding has important implications for building design by acknowledging a greater 'permeability' in the connection between internal and ambient conditions than much modern orthodoxy would allow. The distinction between the 'selective' and 'exclusive' modes is precisely based on the degree of this permeability of the building envelope.

Humphreys' work revealed another important relationship between people, climate, comfort and the nature of buildings when he discovered that there is far less tolerance of variations of temperature in air-conditioned buildings than in those which he called, in a felicitous term, 'free-running'. That is a building that mediates between the internal and external environments solely through the capability of its form and fabric. Again, this is a characterisation of the nature of 'selective' design.

Selective design and comfort

The idea of 'selective' design rests upon the understanding of a building as a system of interrelated and interacting elements.[4] The form, fabric, materials, mechanical systems of a building, and the controls that operate upon them are located within a naturally occurring climate with all of its seasonal and diurnal variations of solar radiation, temperature, humidity, wind speed and direction, variations of ambient light, and so forth. This is then inhabited by human activity that creates a complex set of demands for space and environment that the building has to satisfy. Although buildings are primarily made to meet functional, social and cultural needs, it is important to recognise that the occupants of buildings also play a vital role in the operation of the 'environmental system'. In addition to their specific needs for comfort, which become parameters of the system, the occupants of a building are frequently involved in the operation of the system through their interventions to adjust the fabric – by opening windows, drawing blinds and the like – and by their operation of plant, setting heating controls, switching lights, and so forth. This, again, is a defining characteristic of a 'selective' building.

Environmental control and comfort

A number of years ago, a research study was undertaken by the Cambridge University School of Architecture in which four fundamental questions were posed about the internal environment in a group of school buildings:[5]

- What is the potential for variation of environmental conditions offered within a building, and what influences it?
- To what extent do the occupants of buildings take active steps to modify their environment, and under what stimulus does this occur?
- How wide is the range of environmental conditions tolerated?
- Does this 'toleration' demand changes in activities?

The studies showed that great emphasis was placed by the occupants of these buildings – in this case teachers – upon having the ability to exercise control of the environment of their space. Buildings with automatically controlled mechanical plant caused the greatest dissatisfaction. From this observation, it was inferred that the ability to exercise some degree of control over the internal environment might have a crucial bearing upon people's psychological well-being. In those buildings studied that offered some measure of control, the controls were consistently manipulated in response to variations in the internal or external environment. For example, occupants would modify the state of the building by opening windows or adjusting solar control blinds as conditions demanded. They would also often anticipate the effects of changes in the external conditions *before* they had an impact on the internal environment by exercising a kind of 'feed-forward' response. For example, blinds would be closed *before* the sun struck the glazing. Another extremely sophisticated control action was observed when teachers would manipulate the environment of a classroom to create an appropriate ambience for a particular lesson. An interesting correlation was found between the provision of vigorous, well-ventilated conditions and arithmetic lessons, but, in contrast, a cosy, womb-like state was created for story telling to young children. This phenomenon may be observable only in a few building types, for example, it may be less appropriate in an office than in a school, but the observation reveals a level of environmental subtlety that has not been comprehended by orthodox comfort theory.

Environmental diversity: the spatial and temporal dimensions of comfort

The Cambridge studies in school buildings also suggested that the complex phenomenon of comfort has both *spatial* and *temporal* dimensions. In many buildings the diversity of the activities that take place may demand, or in other cases may tolerate, variation of environment from space to space. It may not be necessary to maintain the whole of the interior at the same, uniform conditions. In the case of the schools studied, it was evident that energetic activities such as drama classes or physical education require very different conditions from those necessary for academic study in the classroom. Indeed, many activities could be satisfactorily accommodated in conditions either warmer or cooler than those of a classroom. In other words, they were environmentally less critical. This implies that certain building types should be planned with different environments in different spaces, with space-by-space environmental diversity. But there is a further dimension to the idea of spatial diversity in which single spaces may have simultaneously occurring diversity – and that this may be desirable. It is quite easy to conceive of spaces for many uses in which some people may seek out a sunny area whilst others may, at the same time, prefer to be in the shade. In this way, a single space may simultaneously satisfy the differing needs of individuals or accommodate quite different activities.

From this research, it was possible to make a number of proposals about the design of user-operated control mechanisms. The most important point is that the function and effect of all controls should be easy to understand. This is particularly important in buildings with large numbers of users or with occupants who may only use it infrequently. For example, heating or lighting controls should be clearly identifiable as such and the equipment to which they are connected should be readily apparent. This requires particular care in the location of controls so that they will be used effectively when environmental action is required.

The studies also showed that whenever people feel that they need to adjust the environment in a building, they require a rapid, if not immediate, response to their actions. They respond to unacceptable or inappropriate conditions and need instant relief. Switching on an electric light is an obvious example of such an immediate response. The control of the thermal environment, however, is much more complex. Overheating is often more rapidly relieved by throwing open a window than by adjusting the heating system, even if it has serious consequences for energy consumption. To avoid this the complex interaction between building fabric, plant and controls must be properly understood by the designer and designed with the greatest of care.

Another dimension of the complexity of the environmental control system is that the stimulus to rectify unsatisfactory conditions is more reliable than the subsequent awareness that the conditions which triggered the original action have now passed and that further action needs to be taken to restore the system to its earlier state. The most familiar example is the way in which artificial lighting is frequently left switched on long after the day has brightened. This specific problem may be relatively easily solved, as indeed it frequently is in practice, by the installation of an automatically operated control such as a simple time switch or a more elaborate monitoring device which links the internal light level to a measure of external conditions. However, in the case of a window opened to bring rapid relief from thermal discomfort, such simple, mechanical solutions are less easy to contrive and it may be better to try to make a design that would avoid the need for the initial response. In environmental design, as in many other things, prevention is better than cure.

Mechanical plant: is it intelligent?

In buildings designed in the 'exclusive' mode of environmental control, the case for the predominance of mechanical plant and automatic control systems in the environmental strategy is often justified by arguing that it ensures the efficient use of energy by preventing 'inference' by the occupants. The 'selective' principle proposes that properly designed user control systems can, by utilising the inherent intelligence of occupants, achieve a closer relationship between human environmental needs and the environment that a building provides. In this way, occupant control can also be efficient.

To achieve this, however, it is essential to have a deeper understanding of the processes that occur when a building interacts with the external environment than is required for the design of mechanical plant. For example, a relatively simple calculation of heat loss or gain provides an adequate basis for the design of a heating or cooling system. But the more complex environment of a space in which direct passive solar gains affecting the internal temperature and, hence, reducing or eliminating the contribution required of the mechanical plant must be understood at another level.

An adaptive model for comfort

This appreciation of the complexity of the environment within buildings has been the subject of much research in recent years. Work at the University of Reading by Derek Clements-Croome and Li Baizhan has stated that

Provision of individual control for as many environmental factors as possible makes it possible to eliminate the discrepancy between individual and group responses and thus provide a cost-effective means of increasing productivity. Individual differences concerning the heat balance requirements, as well as thermal preferences, emphasise the need for increased degrees of freedom of individual control of air quality and thermal factors. This is also true of environmental factors.[6]

One of the key developments in research into environmental design theory has been the proposal, made by a number of authors, of an *Adaptive Model* of comfort that allows for the ability of the users of a building to identify and respond to the shortcomings of the environment within a building. Humphreys argued that the Adaptive Model acknowledges that people take a whole range of actions to secure satisfactory conditions and that this adaptability is the central issue in understanding thermal comfort, and in predicting discomfort.[7] His *Adaptive Principle* proposes that

If a change occurs such as to produce discomfort, people react in ways which tend to restore their comfort.

This coincides precisely with the underlying philosophy of 'selective' design and Humphreys' elaboration of his 'Principle' makes a number of specific proposals for design action:

- The environment should be predictable: the occupants should know what to expect. In practice, this means that temperatures reliably should be the same in similar accommodation. This need not exclude seasonal variation if this is to be expected.
- The environment should be 'normal': it should be within the range acceptable within the social circumstance in that society and climate.
- Where people are free to choose their location, it helps if there is plenty of usable thermal variety, then they can choose the places they like suitable for the activity in which they wish to engage. (Watch a cat finding the best place to sleep.) The same principle applies to the design of outdoor spaces. The provision of sunny and shady spaces, sheltered and open

routes, enhances comfort by giving freedom of choice.

- Where people must be at a fixed location, provide them with adequate control of their thermal environment.
- Avoid sudden imposed changes of temperature.

Humphreys summarised the basis of his work in a simple and elegant schematic model indicating the principal parameters of dynamic equilibrium between a person and the external environment (Figure 4.3).

Complementary work by Nick Baker and Mark Standeven,

4.3 Model of 'dynamic equilibrium' (after Humphreys 1995).

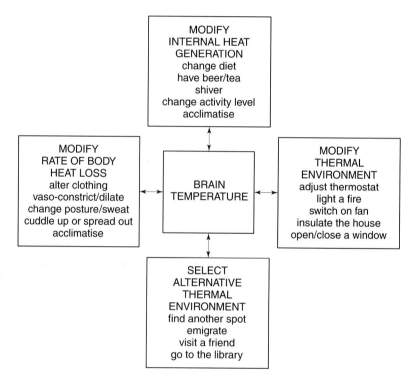

carried out at the University of Cambridge, has formalised the notion of environmental diversity and adaptation in a model of *Adaptive Opportunity*.[8] This establishes a clear hierarchy of relationships derived from the propensity of living organisms to exhibit *irritability* (Figure 4.4), which is defined as 'responsiveness to change in the environment by complex adaptive activity'. The argument then suggests that 'the experience of non-neutral thermal conditions cannot automatically lead to thermal dissatisfaction'. Stress only occurs when the stimulus exceeds the limits of the adaptive opportunity, or, it is hypothesised, when the subject fails to appreciate that adaptive opportunity is available. Following Humphreys' argument about the levels of tolerance exhibited by the occupants of buildings of different environmental character, Baker and Standeven suggest that when the cause of a particular environmental stimulus is known and understood, such as a sunbeam or a draught on a windy day, people are more tolerant and the adaptive zone is, thus, extended. The term 'cognitive tolerance' has been coined to describe this phenomenon. Conversely, it is suggested that where the subject cannot identify the cause of an environmental condition or does not understand it, stress will result. Three simple principles summarise the implications of this work:

- Limit the extremes of thermal conditions by the inherent properties of the building.
- Provide an adaptive opportunity by environmental variety and user-friendly building controls.
- Allow visual access to outdoor climatic conditions and a simple 'readable' architectural design.

4.4 Model of 'adaptive opportunity' (after Baker and Standeven 1995).

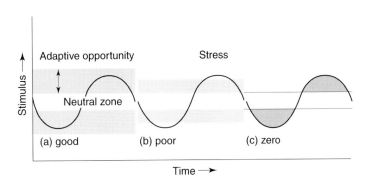

Design context and comfort

These principles of comfort in selective buildings are applicable wherever the building might be located. As Humphreys observed, however, specific comfort temperatures, and, it is suggested here, by extrapolation other environmental factors, are conditioned by the characteristics of the prevailing climate, by the cultural conditions of the society and by the nature of the building itself. In particular, whether the building depends upon mechanical services for its primary environmental control.

As Humphreys' early studies show, the best correlate for internal design temperatures is the mean prevailing outdoor air temperature. Figure 4.5 shows the accuracy of the correlation showing how, in warm climates, the neutral temperature may be established directly from the outdoor temperature. The cultural influences upon perceived comfort are not fully understood, but there is ample evidence to suggest that within certain limits winter indoor temperatures are likely to be conditioned more by established practice than by any particular correlation with the external climate. For example, North American design temperatures are typically higher than those accepted in Europe in similar climatic conditions. There is also clear evidence that standards become self-fulfilling, in that people adapt to what is provided and report it to be comfortable. Humphreys' work shows that *free-running* buildings, which are precisely characteristic of selective design, allow a wider range of tolerance of indoor temperature variation than do 'exclusive' designs, in which mechanical plant is in operation for either heating or cooling.

4.5 Correlation of internal design temperature and mean prevailing outdoor temperature (after Humphreys 1995).

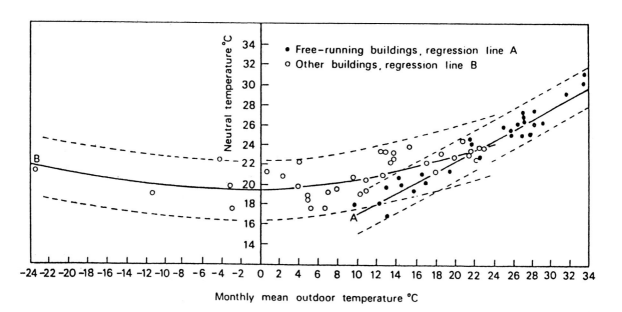

Studies of 'selective' comfort in practice

The relationship between theory and practice in architecture is complex. It may be argued that the best practice must be informed by the application of coherent theory. On the other hand, practice plays a vital role in testing the validity of theory and, hence, in its refinement and further development. The propositions of selective design were given their first test in the design and construction of Netley Abbey Infants' School at Netley, Hampshire, on the South Coast of England.[9] The Architects' Department of Hampshire County Council collaborated with a research team at the University of Cambridge to translate the first statement of 'selective' principles into guidelines for the design of low-energy school buildings.

4.6 Netley Abbey Infants' School, Netley, Hampshire, UK: cross-section. Architect: Hampshire County Architects' Department.

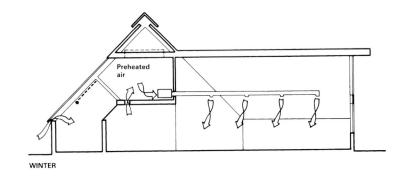

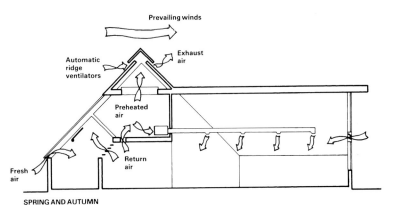

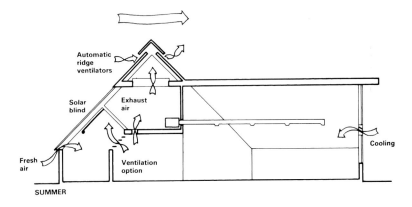

The essence of the Netley design was the definition of distinct zones of environmental control (Figure 4.6). One, which was relatively precisely defined, consisted of the principal teaching spaces. Another, in which greater environmental diversity was acceptable, included spaces such as the conservatory, which occupies the entire south-east face of the building. In addition, a principal role in the environmental control processes was assigned to the occupants, who were offered the opportunity to control the operation of heating and artificial lighting in response to their perception of need. Since its completion in 1985, the building has operated in this mode and detailed monitoring carried out between 1985 and 1987 showed that it provided a high-quality environment with great economy of energy.

The close collaboration between the research team and designers almost certainly contributed to the success of the design, but the true test of theory must come when it is applied more widely. Two other buildings in the UK allow us to examine the adoption of selective design to very different circumstances.[10]

The School of Engineering, The Queen's Building, at De Montfort University, Leicester (1993), is remarkable for the extent to which it makes use of 'passive' processes of environmental control (Figure 4.7). Its most reported and architecturally most conspicuous element is the use of natural ventilation in its principal spaces, using tall vent shafts that rise through the building to emerge high above the roofline. In addition, the building places much reliance upon its occupants to control its systems and it is this aspect of the design that is of concern here.

The first point to note is that the building houses a diverse set of functions and, hence, of spaces and environments, including large lecture rooms, seminar rooms, teaching laboratories, research laboratories, and academic and administrative offices.

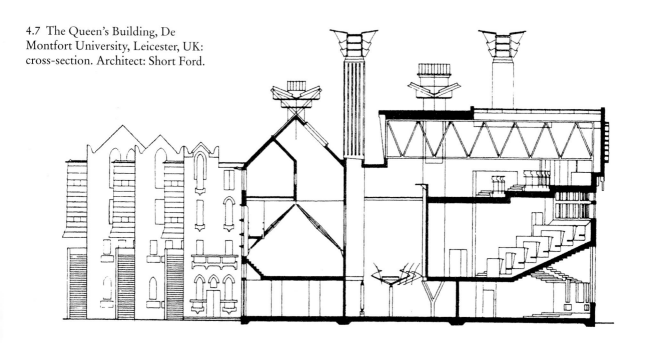

4.7 The Queen's Building, De Montfort University, Leicester, UK: cross-section. Architect: Short Ford.

Consequently, the users of the building – academic and administrative staff, students, and technicians – develop a complex experience of the spaces they inhabit. For example, a lecturer will move from a personal office to a seminar room, then to a teaching laboratory, then to a lecture room, and so on. A student might on one day attend a series of lectures and on another work entirely in a laboratory. Sometimes people will work in large groups, others in small groups and at others may work alone. All these conditions redefine the occupants' relationship to the building and, hence, their role in its environmental processes.

Observations made on a brief visit to the building shortly after its completion indicated the complexity of occupant control in such large institutional buildings. Achieving efficient control of artificial lighting is a familiar problem in many buildings and a number of instances of this were encountered in the School of Engineering. One of these occurred in a large, roof-lit mechanical engineering laboratory where all of the artificial lighting was in use at a time when only a small area of the space was in use by a group of technicians. When the level of daylight was measured, it was insufficient for carrying out precision work at machine tools, but the entire artificial lighting installation was in use because the design and location of the switching made it difficult to control localised areas of the space. A variation of this problem was encountered in an electrical engineering laboratory. Here great care had been devoted to the design of the daylighting of the space. Light shelves at the windows provided a uniform distribution of light while protecting workplaces at the perimeter from glare. The occupant-controlled artificial lighting consisted of two systems, one providing general background light as a substitute for daylight, the other task-lighting at the individual workplaces. The background lighting was controlled from a single position in the entrance lobby to the laboratory while the task lighting was individually controlled. On the visit, all of the lights – background and task – were in use at a time when there were only three students in the space. The daylight level, which was tested by simply switching off the artificial lighting, was at the time more than adequate as background.

The important point that these two observations raise is that of the 'legibility' of controls in user-controlled environments. This is partly a matter of their location within or relative to the space and to the devices they operate. Unless the function of a control is clear to the user of the building, particularly one who is an intermittent occupant of the space, it is unlikely that it will be operated intelligently.

Similar problems arise with other kinds of control. Even a relatively familiar device such as a thermostatic radiator valve may fail to operate as expected. This was the case in a small private office where the occupant was responding to overheating on a winter's day by opening a window rather than by adjusting the heating control. In such a large and complex building containing such spatial and functional diversity as the School of Engineering, and this is typical of many modern institutional buildings, there will inevitably be a corresponding diversity of control systems. This means that the users have constantly to change their perception of the way in which the environmental control system operates as they move about the building. This poses questions of 'architectural semantics' that have, as yet, been barely identified and which have a crucial bearing upon the successful adoption of selective design principles.

A second project that casts yet more light upon this question is The Friary at Maldon in Essex, also completed in 1993 (Figure 4.8). It consists of two buildings, the larger of which contains a branch of the County Library on the ground floor with two floors of offices above. The smaller building is a daycare centre for the mentally handicapped. Both buildings incorporate the principles of selective design with a clear response to orientation in the sizing of the windows. The internal environment is free-running in the summer months with natural lighting and ventilation. Auxiliary heating is provided by a simple gas-fired system with high-efficiency modular boilers and room radiators controlled by thermostatic valves. A low-energy artificial lighting system is user-controlled and locally switched.

4.8 The Friary, Maldon, Essex, UK: cross-section. Architect: Greenberg and Hawkes.

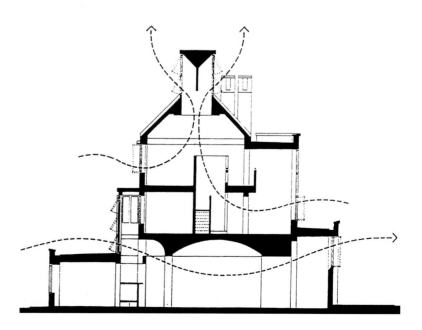

The occupants operate all of the mechanisms for environmental control. In the case of a library building, control is usually exercised by the staff, the librarians, who are present in the building throughout the day, rather than by the readers, who normally stay for a relatively short time. In a sense, the staff acts as monitors of the environment on behalf of the other users – as 'human thermostats'. In a study carried out after completion, the staff, when interviewed, declared that they found the building easy to understand and operate and that the environment it provided was comfortable. On a warm summer's day, the building was described by both staff and readers interviewed as 'fresh' or 'cool'.

On this evidence, the building may be considered a success. There were, however, a number of interesting oddities in the way in which it was actually being operated that further illustrate the complexity of the process of environmental control, particularly when it is substantially in the hands of the users of a building. Many of these, as in the case of The Queen's Building, followed from the 'legibility', or more precisely from the 'illegibility', of the building and its systems as perceived by the users, and from the importance of the smallest details of the design in facilitating this understanding and easy operation.

At Maldon, an example of this was the perception that the adjustable blinds to the principal windows were part of the building's security system, not its environmental controls, and were, therefore, drawn in the evening when the building was closed for the night and opened when the staff arrived in the morning. The most significant discrepancy between the designers' expectations and the operation of the building was in the control of the artificial lighting. The building was carefully designed to provide a high level of natural light throughout the library space. On a bright summer's day, however, the research study was surprised to discover that all of the artificial lighting was in use. This was explained as being the library authorities' policy of operating the lighting at all times to ensure that there would be satisfactory levels for partially sighted users.

A number of general observations may be made from the experience of these two buildings. First is to remind ourselves that a building is primarily a *social* system, that its *raison d'être* is to provide a setting for human activity. People go to buildings to work, teach, be taught, borrow a book and so on, and these purposes are their principal activities. The control of the environment, by whatever means, must be a secondary concern. If, as argued above, the user has a vital role to play in environmental control, designers must have a new understanding of the principles involved if they are to achieve fully effective designs. The following points should be observed:

- Identify the uses that the building will accommodate.
- Make a detailed schedule of all of the activities, accounting for the number of users participating in each, the composition of the group and the times at which each activity may occur.
- Design all controls, whether on fabric or plant, to be simple and clearly associated with the devices they operate and locate them so that are easily and appropriately used.
- Ensure that the users, and particularly those who within the social system that inhabits the building are most likely to exercise environmental control, have a complete understanding of the way in which the building is to be operated.

References

1 Victor Olgyay, *Design with Climate: Bioclimatic Approach to Architectural Regionalism*, Princeton University Press, Princeton, NJ, 1963.

2 R. G. Hopkinson, *Architectural Physics: Lighting*, HMSO, London, 1964.

3 Michael A. Humphreys, *Field Studies of Thermal Comfort Compared and Applied*. CP76/75, Building Research Establishment, Garston.

4 Dean Hawkes, 'The theoretical basis of comfort in "selective" environments', in *The Environmental Tradition: Studies in the Architecture of Environment*, E & FN Spon, London, 1996, pp. 28–35.

5 Diane Haigh, 'User response in environmental control', in Dean Hawkes and Janet Owers (eds), *The Architecture of Energy*, Construction Press/Longman, Harlow, 1982.

6 Derek Clements-Croome and Li Baizhan, 'Impact of indoor environment on productivity', in *Workplace Comfort Forum*, RIBA, London, 1995.

7 M. A. Humphreys, 'What causes discomfort?', in *Workplace Comfort Forum*, RIBA, London, 1995.

8 Nick Baker and Mark Standeven, 'Adaptive opportunity as a comfort parameter', in *Workplace Comfort Forum*, RIBA, London, 1995. Also Nick Baker, 'The irritable occupant: recent developments in thermal comfort theory', *Architectural Research Quarterly*, 2, 1996.

9 Dean Hawkes, 'Building Study: Netley Abbey Infants' School, Hampshire, UK', *Architects' Journal*, 1988; repr. in Hawkes, *Environmental Tradition*, pp. 130–41

10 Dean Hawkes, 'The user's role in environmental control: some reflections on theory in practice', in Derek Clements-Croome (ed.), *Naturally Ventilated Buildings: Buildings for the Senses, the Economy and Society*, E & FN Spon, London, 1997.

5　Typology in environmental design

Ultimately, we can say that type is the very idea of architecture, that which is closest to its essence. In spite of changes, it has always imposed itself on the 'feelings and reason' as the principle of architecture and of the city . . . Typology is an element that plays its own role in constituting form; it is a constant.[1]

As this quotation from Aldo Rossi suggests, the idea of 'type' plays an important role in architectural theory and most particularly in addressing the question of the relationship between established knowledge and the production of new designs. For Rossi, typology was the instrument through which he developed his 'Critique of Naive Functionalism', in which he argued for the authority of type in relation to function.

I believe that any explanation of urban artefacts in terms of function must be rejected if the issue is to elucidate their structure and formation . . . Thus, one thesis of this study, in its effort to affirm the value of architecture in the analysis of the city, is the denial of the explanation of urban artefacts in terms of function. I maintain, on the contrary, that far from being illuminating, this explanation is regressive because it impedes us from studying forms and knowing the world of architecture according to its true laws.

Citing the work of Bronislaw Malinowski, who proposed that 'the integral function of the object must be taken into account when the various phases of its technological construction and the elements of its structure are studied',[2] Rossi protested that 'The question of "for what purpose?" ends up as a simple justification that prevents an analysis of what is real.'

Rossi's preoccupation is with the *study* of, in his terminology, the urban artefact. It is implicit in his argument for the primacy of type over function that the origin of new designs will, in some way, derive from the understanding and transformation of type and not from the 'logic' of *form follows function* as process. None the less, he is forced to acknowledge that:

functionalism has had great success in the world of architecture, and those who have been educated in this discipline over the past fifty years can detach themselves from it only with difficulty. One ought to inquire into how it has actually determined modern architecture, and still inhibits its progressive evolution today . . .

One of the objections to the role of typology in the production of architecture is that it is inappropriate in an age of science and technology. It was only necessary to refer to pre-existing models in an age of craft, in the absence of the general laws of explanation, which the scientific process has now delivered. But how does this proposition stand up to critical examination?

One of the most penetrating commentaries on this point of view was made by Alan Colquhoun in 'Typology and design method' (1967).[3] There he reviewed the proposition made by Tomas Maldonado, who was one of the leading figures in the 'Design Methods' school in the 1960s, that until it becomes possible to classify and quantify all the parameters of a design problem, 'it might be necessary to use a typology of forms to fill the gap . . . Although he regards this as a provisional solution . . .'. Colquhoun argued, citing the work of two significant avant-garde designers of the 1960s, Yona Friedman and Yannis Xenakis, that there was a substantial body of evidence in the literature of modern architecture that demonstrated that statements of functional requirements, no matter how extensive they might be, can never fully determine the nature of a design. No matter what the problem might be, Colquhoun concluded that in architectural design 'Recourse to some kind of typological model is even more necessary.'

One of the most cogent attempts to connect the functionalist arguments of the design methodologists with the systematic application of typology in the design process was made by Lionel March in 'The logic of design and the question of value' (1976).[4] In this he examined the problem of the origin of 'the first design proposal', which, in the accounts of design methodology, would in some way emerge from the precise, functional statement of the problem. In his 'P-D-I' model of design, March argued that

In this iterative procedure, it is assumed that certain characteristics are sought in a design . . . and that on the basis of previous knowledge and some general presuppositions or models of possibilities, a design proposal is put forward. Such a speculative design cannot be determined logically . . . It can only be inferred conditionally upon our state of knowledge and available evidence.

The 'previous knowledge and some general suppositions or models of possibilities', to which March referred, is, almost inevitably, embodied in some pre-existing type. By analogy with concepts in biology, he distinguished between *genotype* and *phenotype*, the former being the characterisation of the general properties of a population, and the latter being an individual instance. This distinction nicely establishes the relationship between the *general* characteristics of a building type and the *specific* nature of any individual building, and so to acknowledge that the generalities of typology do not inhibit the realisation of a proper response to the circumstances and situation of a design. Incidentally, this proposition is remarkably close to Rossi's definition of 'the concept of type as something that is permanent and complex, a logical principle that is prior to form and that constitutes it'.

The function of typology in the field of environmental design was explored by Dean Hawkes in 'Type, norms and habit in environmental design' (1996).[5] There an analysis of the development of the British office building, from the end of the nineteenth century to the 1970s, was used to demonstrate both the dominance of the prevailing *stereotype* in the design of such buildings and the nature of the evolutionary process. The essay demonstrated that in the design of utilitarian buildings such as offices, reliance is often placed in determining a viable environmental strategy upon reference to the current 'best' solution in initiating the process. The validity of the argument was later reinforced by the replacement of the deep-plan office type that dominated British practice in the 1970s and which concluded the sequence analysed, by the atrium form which became the standard, 'stereotypical', solution in the 1980s. However, the great value of *typology*, as opposed to the singular type, in the production of new designs is that it constitutes a store of alternatives from which the starting point for the development of a promising solution might be drawn.

In his important book *The Evolution of Designs: Biological Analogy in Architecture and the Applied Arts* (1979), Philip Steadman pointed out that most typologies in architecture, as in the natural sciences, are empirically derived from the classification of identifiable populations:

The emergence of archaeology as an organised scholarly enterprise in the eighteenth century, as well as accumulated evidence from travellers' accounts and foreign expeditions, had provided architectural writers with an increasing mass of quite disorganised material on the variety of historical and national or local styles in building. Any comprehensive theory of architecture would have to set this material in order, organise it into some classificatory scheme, draw some lessons which would be useful for a modern 'style', for future architecture.[6]

In architecture, typologies are derived from analysis and interpretation of the stock of existing buildings. Durand's *Recueil et Parallele des Edifices* (Paris, 1801) is just such a taxonomy, with plans drawn to a common scale, of historical buildings arranged, according to functional categories. Steadman observes that this is 'like nothing so much as the specimens for some work of natural history or geology'.

Making reference to actual instances remains one of the most potent ways in which architects can begin the process of fashioning new designs. In communicating the principles of selective design, some contemporary projects are presented in Chapter 7 that illustrate themes related to the Selective Environment. However, developments in architectural science, and particularly in the capability of computer-based calculation methods, make it possible to generate typologies to demonstrate precise relationships between generic form and specific aspects of performance. Chapter 6 presents the outcome of such a study that refers to the contrasted climates of London and Lagos in demonstrating the connection between climate and design.

References

1 Aldo Rossi, *The Architecture of the City*, MIT Press, Cambridge, MA, 1982.

2 Bronislaw Malinowski, *A Scientific Theory of Culture and Other Essays*, University of North Carolina Press, Chapel Hill, 1944; cited in Rossi, *Architecture of the City*.

3 Alan Colquhoun, 'Typology and design method', in *Essays in Architectural Criticism: Modern Architecture and Historical Change*, MIT Press, Cambridge, MA, 1981.

4 Lionel March, 'The logic of design and the question of value', in Lionel March (ed.), *The Architecture of Form*, Cambridge University Press, Cambridge, 1976.

5 Dean Hawkes, 'Type, norms and habit in environmental design', in March (ed.), *Architecture of Form*; repr. in revised form in Dean Hawkes, *The Environmental Tradition: Studies in the Architecture of Environment*, E & FN Spon, London, 1996, pp. 46–55.

6 Philip Steadman, *The Evolution of Designs: Biological Analogy in Architecture and the Applied Arts*, Cambridge University Press, Cambridge, 1979.

6 Generic models for selective design

Elementary mathematical models are an excellent source of inquiry . . . they may help clear away some of the misleading 'rules-of-thumb' which frequently lurk behind design decisions, and they may help to replace these by more cautious generalisations, but, be warned – these may be equally misleading if results and conclusions are extrapolated beyond the simplifying assumptions of the original model.[1]

Following the argument for the function of typology in the production of architectural designs, this chapter presents a *typology for selective design*. This is based upon generic spaces whose environmental properties are explicitly demonstrated using data derived from the LT Method of environmental analysis developed by Baker and Steemers.[2] This has been incorporated into a computer model that describes typical spaces that can be combined to construct approximate representations of possible building designs of, in the terminology of Chapter 5, a 'genotype' or first design proposal. The environmental performance of these may then be investigated further by varying orientation and aspects of their façade design. It is not the aim here to present a comprehensive tool for designers, rather it is to show how the typological approach may be used to establish certain fundamental parameters of environmental response. The calculations have been made for the contrasted climates of Lagos and London.

The climates of Lagos and London exhibit the essential difference between equatorial and temperate conditions and the worked examples of typological design serve the additional purpose of illustrating the nature of the connection between climate and architecture. The principal characteristics of the climate in each city are summarised in Table 6.1. Comparative sunpath diagrams, mean monthly temperatures and incident solar irradiances are given in Figures 6.1–6.6.

6.1 Sunpath diagram for London, UK.

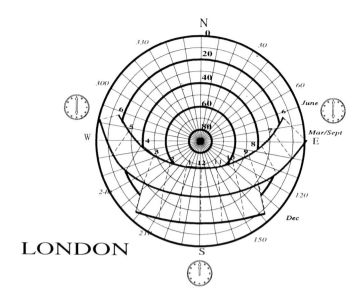

LONDON

6.2 Sunpath diagram for Lagos, Nigeria.

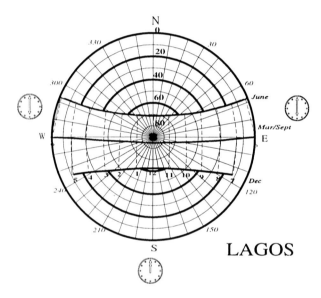

LAGOS

6.3 Monthly mean temperatures for London.

6.4 Monthly mean temperatures for Lagos.

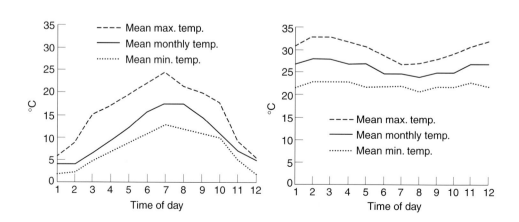

6.5 Incident solar radiation for vertical surfaces for London.

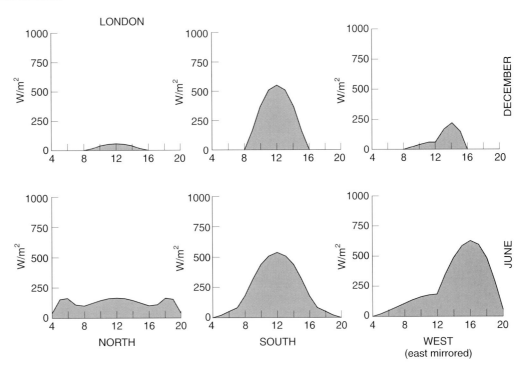

6.6 Incident solar radiation for vertical surfaces for Lagos.

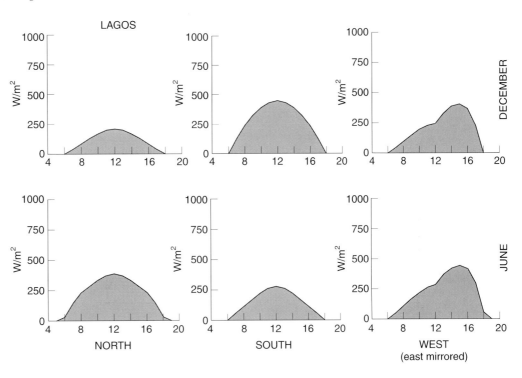

Table 6.1
Climate comparison between London and Lagos.

	London	Lagos
General	Both seasonal and diurnal variations	Slight seasonal and diurnal variations. High night-time temperatures and humidity
Wind	Wind speeds are low to moderate and most frequently west to south-westerly. The coldest winds are from the north-east	Calm conditions are uncommon (1–3%), but about 50–60% with light westerly winds. During daytime hours the winds are predominantly north to north-easterly at the time of the northern winter, changing to south to south-westerly in the corresponding summer
Temperature	Average diurnal range in winter is < 3°C and < 6°C in summer. Average winter daily minimum is 2.3°C, and average summer daily maximum is 21.6°C. The average annual range is therefore > 18°C	Annual range is very small, but the maximum mean monthly variation is marked. A cooling effect due to rains is evident from May to September, and the cloud cover almost halves the diurnal range at this time
Sunshine and cloud	High occurrence of cloudy skies. Solar radiation is reduced by atmospheric pollution, especially on hot days. Summer averages 7 hours of sunshine, while the winter average is 1.5 hours	Solar radiation is not very high – being similar to New Orleans or Athens – due to the high moisture content of the air and the cloud cover during the wet season, and the dust and smoke pollution during the dry season. There is very high cloud cover during August
Humidity	Generally only moderate humidity, although high levels may be experienced for a short period in the summer months	In the coastal regions of Nigeria such as Lagos, June–October has monthly mean humidities of > 90%, with lower levels between January and April

The typological model presented here is based on the definition of a number of distinct conditions of space, each defined by its location within the overall configuration of a complete building. These are as follows:

- Corner spaces with glazing in adjacent walls: long side north or south (Figure 6.7a).
- Corner spaces with glazing in adjacent walls – long side east or west (Figure 6.7b).
- Central spaces – not overshadowed (Figure 6.7c).
- Central spaces – overshadowed (Figure 6.7d).

It is possible to construct descriptions and, hence, environmental assessments of a large number of possible buildings from the combination of these into specific forms, which may be defined by the conditions of site and programme given in any specific design (Figure 6.8).

6.7 Environmental typology – room types: (a) corner spaces with glazing in adjacent walls – long side north or south; (b) corner spaces with glazing in adjacent walls – long side east or west; (c) central spaces – not overshadowed; (d) central spaces – overshadowed.

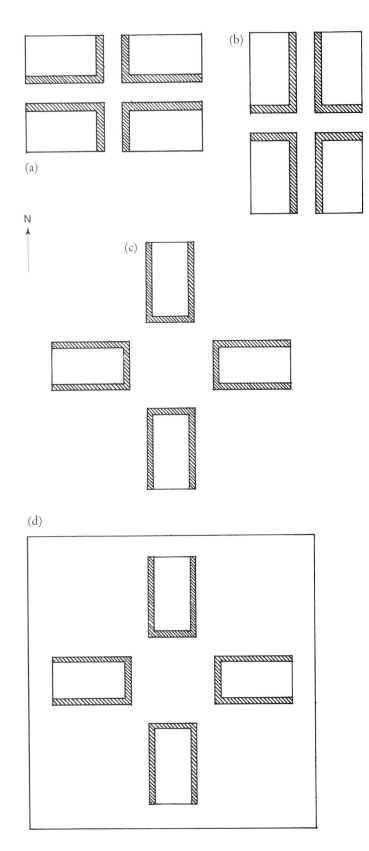

6.8 Alternative plan forms: (a) pavilion – shallow plan; (b) courtyard; (c) pavilion – 'T'-shape; (d) pavilion – deep plan.

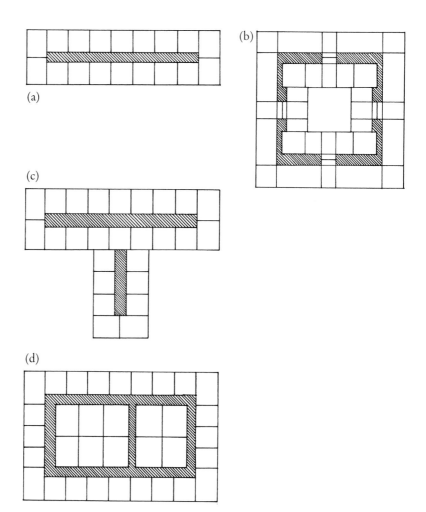

(a)

(b)

(c)

(d)

The application of the data is demonstrated in the studies that follow. A generic building plan, in the form of a simple courtyard, defines the locations of the room types (Figure 6.9). Each is then evaluated environmentally for the climate conditions of London and Lagos. For each room type, a matrix of energy demand has been calculated. This differentiates between orientation – north, south, east, west – and the percentage of glazing in the façade (15–95%). The energy demand is expressed in terms of total annual energy use for the room in megawatt/hours (MW h). The value for each case, that is room type, orientation, glazing area, is indicated by the density of tone, on a scale from 1.0 to 21.5 MW h. The key to the scale in Figure 6.9 is shown in Figure 6.10. Other simple codes indicate cases where discomfort may occur from glare or overheating in non-air-conditioned cases and those cases where air-conditioning will be required to achieve comfort. For the complete set of data charts, see Appendix (Figures A1–A12).

6.9 Building data chart.

GENERIC BUILDING PLAN WITH % GLAZING KEY

Building type: Non-domestic
Occupancy 11 hours/day and 5 days/week
(e.g. office)

Spatial form
Room height = 3 metres
Cross section = 15 metres
Area of data sets = 45 metres squared

Glazing
Glazing Bars and frame = 20%
Glazing type = double
Work plane height = 0.9 metres
Reflectances: ceiling = 0.7, walls = 0.4, floor = 0.25

Thermal transmittance
U values (W/metre square K)
external wall = 0.35, roof = 0.35, window = 2.85

Lighting
Lighting power 12 W/m square
Overcast skies
Illuminance datum = 300 lux

Heating: UK
Heating set point = 20°C
Heating efficiency = 0.6
Occupancy and equipment = 30 W/metre squared

Ventilation and cooling: UK
Fresh air: fan energy = 0.027 MWh/metre square
Air conditioning: fan energy = 0.075 MWh/metre square

Heating: West Africa
None

Ventilation and cooling: West Africa
Air conditioning: cooling set point = 21°C

45 metre squared
Corner Data Set:
adjacent glazing asymmetrical:
dominant South or North the East or West

adjacent glazing
asymmetrical:
dominant West or East

45 metres squared
Internal Data Set group: no glazing

45 metres squared
Central Data Set group
consisting of:

36 metres squared Central Data Set
group

9 metres squared Central
Data Set group corridor or
deep plan zone 1.5 metres
wide

36 metres squared set within courtyard
(or shaded by adjacent buildings)

N

Data Sets show equivalent % glazing of elevation

15%   35%   55%   75%   95%

6.10 Energy demand data chart (MW h/total area).

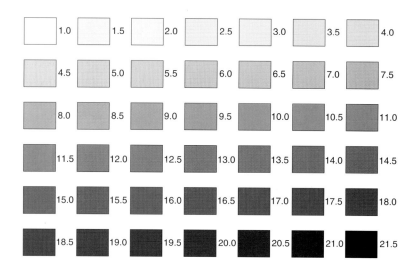

Worked example

The use of the data contained in these charts can be illustrated by the following worked examples of design for both London and Lagos. If one takes the case of a simple rectangular block with a central corridor, the form of which is typical for many commercial buildings (Figure 6.11), it is possible to explore the effects of the variables of orientation and glazed area in the search for the form with the lowest annual energy consumption.

6.11 Worked example: generic plan.

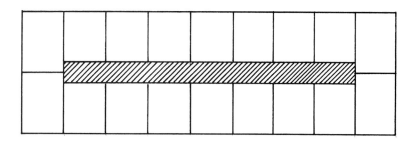

When the data charts for Lagos are examined, it is discovered that for the central spaces that constitute the majority of the building, the north and south orientations have lower energy demand than those east and west, and that in this equatorial climate lower glazing ratios are better. The dominance of the central spaces means that where possible, the orientation of the building should be determined by optimising them. The end or corner spaces should then be designed to minimise their energy demands and, of primary importance, to maximise comfort in them. In this case, the only available variable is the area of glazing. If the space were to be glazed on its two adjacent sides, it would have a higher energy demand than the central spaces. In view of this, it may be decided to glaze on only one side, preferably the north or south, which would give it a performance similar to that of the central spaces. Examination of the data charts (Appendix) shows that the minimum energy demand for unobstructed central spaces, oriented north or south, will be achieved when the glazing area is low, i.e. 15%. A model of the resultant built form can now be constructed (Figure 6.12).

6.12 Worked example: Lagos design. Orientation: long façades, north–south; glazing, 15%.

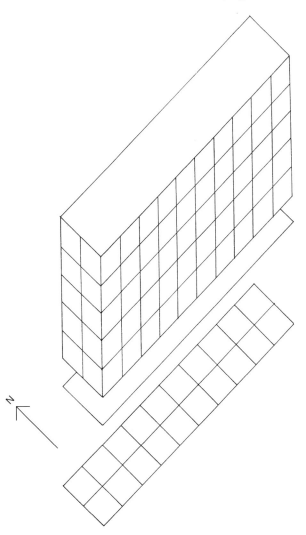

Turning to London, the data charts shows that with careful design, it is possible to avoid the use of air-conditioning in a building of this form. Also, as would be expected in a temperate climate, the total energy consumption would be lower than in Lagos. The question of orientation is less clear cut, however, because of the relative absence of extremes in exposure to solar radiation.

Proceeding as before, the London data charts (Appendix) show that the central spaces in a north–south-oriented block exhibit a wider variation of energy demand, relative to each other and in response to the glazing ratio, than those with an east–west orientation. At lower glazing ratios (15–35%), however, these are less marked. End or corner spaces, particularly those facing south, are more exposed and require careful consideration to avoid overheating. The conclusion is that a building of this form, oriented east–west, should have similar glazing ratios (~35%) in each façade. If the orientation is north–south, the amount of glazing may be different on each elevation, restricted to ≤ 35% to the north, but advantageously increased to the south to benefit from useful solar gains. The model of this form can now be constructed (Figure 6.13).

6.13 Worked example: London design. (a) Orientation: long façades, north–south; glazing: north, 35%; south 55%; (b) orientation: long façades, east–west; glazing: east and west, 35%.

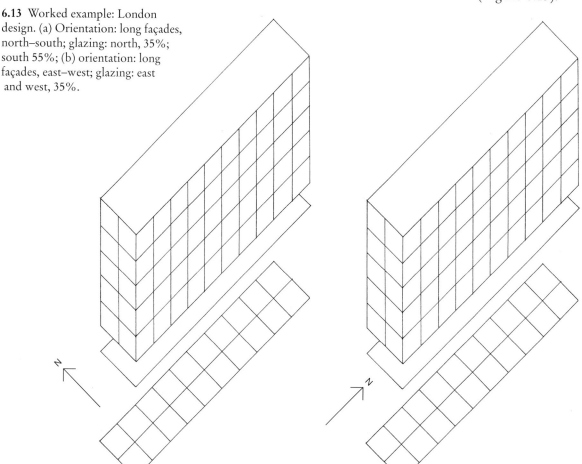

References

1 Lionel March and Philip Steadman, *The Geometry of Environment*, RIBA, London, 1971.

2 N. V. Baker and K. Steemers, *The LT Method v 2.0*, Cambridge Architectural Research and The Martin Centre for Architectural and Urban Studies, Cambridge, 1994.

7   Case studies

The 'generic' studies of Chapter 6 are concerned with the specifically mathematical relationship between built form and energy demand. As architectural representation, these forms are deliberately 'primitive' to present essential technical information with clarity. We are convinced that it is essential that architectural design should be founded on a grasp of relationships of this kind. Where the success of a building can be predicted with a degree of mathematical precision, it would be unwise to ignore relatively simple tools of this kind. On the other hand, as has been consistently stressed, the design of a building is too complex to be reduced to such mechanistic formulations alone. For this reason, a series of 'Case Studies' of buildings is presented, the buildings of which, in their environmental intentions, conform to selective principles.

A 'selective' building has an intimate relationship with its immediate environment. That environment is explicitly and objectively characterised by the physical description of the climate of the place and by the set of physical conditions within which comfort will be achieved. However, as argued above, these parameters are always subject to elaboration and interpretation in the light of the 'cultural pressures' that bear upon the production of any work of architecture. In choosing 'Case Study' buildings to show how theory might be translated into practice, designs have been looked for that operate in the domains of both rigorous technological logic and the subtleties of cultural pressure.

From the very earliest days, the debate about the nature of environmentally responsible architecture has included a strand of what may be termed 'environmental determinism'. The argument is made that the new demands, which follow from the need to reduce energy consumption and environmental impact, will produce a 'new' architecture. By developing an environmental reinterpretation of the modernist dictum that 'form follows function', it is proposed that architecture will aspire to a new objectivity.

Often this argument is extended to make an appeal to a kind of populism. In their influential writings on 'green architecture',

Brenda and Robert Vale have proposed a formula for a 'green aesthetic' in which the buildings of, for example, the Moravian settlements in England and those of the Shakers in the USA are offered as exemplars of the virtues of honest simplicity:

An architecture that would look at buildings with a similar judgement, and determine beauty through performance might not be so bad. For too long architecture has been dragged into the inaccessibility of fine art . . .[1]

Selective design, by its nature, adopts a fundamentally different position on the question of the source of architectural form and language. Whilst much common ground is shared with the Vales, our position is more accommodating, more inclusive, in relating the demands of environmental principle to the complex ground of cultural pressure upon which architecture operates. We are convinced that the case for environmental responsibility must be located as an essential element of the wider theoretical debate in architecture. The Case Study buildings allow us to illustrate our position and, specifically, through the consideration of the nature of their enclosing envelopes.

Selective envelope

In common parlance in English, the word *envelope*, borrowed from the French, means 'Any enclosing covering; a wrapper.'[2] In its architectural usage, the *building envelope* is, at first sight, a quite straightforward adaptation of the generic term. It 'encloses', 'covers' or 'wraps' the volumes that constitute a building, just like the paper of a parcel. Further consideration begins to show that the analogy is less precise, and a detailed examination reveals that the term embraces, perhaps conceals, questions of great complexity. We will try to elucidate some of these and, as so often, the best place to begin is in the past. If we step back to the sixteenth century and look at two great buildings of the European Renaissance, one in Italy and the other in England, we may establish some of the fundamentals.

Andrea Palladio's Villa Rotonda near Vicenza (Figure 7.1) is, perhaps most importantly, an essay in geometrical form and mathematical proportion, through which a complex set of philosophical ideals is expressed.[3] But it also was conceived as a practical dwelling, and continues to fulfil this function today. In this more pragmatic territory, which was itself an explicit preoccupation of Palladio himself, as his *I quattro libri dell'architettura* (1570) clearly shows, the villa may be interpreted as a sophisticated essay in the design of the building

7.1 Andrea Palladio, Villa Rotonda, Vicenza, Italy (1566–67).

envelope. Its enclosing walls and roof operate as a precisely calculated boundary between the climate of the Veneto and the more moderate environment within. The constructional methods of the time and situation of the Villa Rotonda dictated that the enclosing walls be built from load-bearing masonry and that these would be punctured by window and door openings. This is the technology of 'hole-in-wall' architecture. In mediating between the external climate and internal environment, the question was to determine the sizes of these openings to fulfil the demands of lighting, ventilation and temperature control. In *I quattro libri dell'architettura*, Palladio gave precise formulas to meet these needs.[4]

The second historical example is Hardwick Hall in Derbyshire, an almost contemporary house designed by Robert Smythson in England (Figure 7.2).[5] The point we want to make in the present discussion, by comparing these two buildings, is that a broadly similar technology, that of load-bearing, hole-in-wall construction was capable of allowing conspicuously distinctive responses to the different climatic and cultural conditions of Renaissance Italy and Jacobean England. Hardwick has been colloquially characterised as 'Hardwick Hall, more glass than wall', which, whilst not strictly accurate mathematically, is an impression

7.2 Robert Smythson, Hardwick
Hall, Derbyshire, UK (1590–97).

borne out by one's first sight of the building. In temperate
England, the large areas of window bring more light to the interior without suffering thermal penalties in the summer months
and, in spite of their implications for heat loss in winter, the
needs of Jacobean thermal comfort were met by an array of
coal-burning fireplaces located in the massive spine wall running
the entire length of the house.

So we have established that the environmental function of
the building envelope is to act as a mediator, a 'filter', between
inside and out. We have also seen that the relationship of
window to wall, solid to void, is a key variable in achieving a
judicious environmental balance. Importantly, one should note
that the environmental objectives of these two significant buildings find their place, apparently effortlessly, in relation to
complex and comprehensive systems of architectural language
and composition. Questions of function, form and aesthetics
are resolved in a seamless whole, which was the essence of
Renaissance culture.

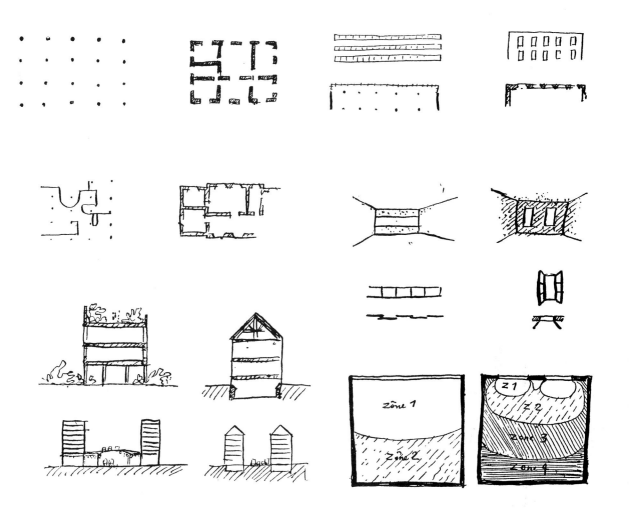

7.3 Le Corbusier, *Cinque points d'une architecture nouvelle* (1926).

'Dom-ino' and mechanisation

In the first decades of the twentieth century, a radically new conception of architecture emerged. This was, partly, the consequence of developments that occurred in the technologies, or, as we prefer, *techniques*,[6] of structure, construction and the mechanisation of environmental control. It was also a product of changes in the relationship of technique to form and language in architecture.[7]

One of the key elements of this transformation was the widespread adoption of a frame of steel or concrete as the primary structural system of a building. The most celebrated argument for the adoption of a frame rather than load-bearing masonry construction was in Le Corbusier's *Cinque points d'une architecture nouvelle* (Figure 7.3).[8] The use of the frame fundamentally changed the whole nature of architectural design. This is clearly shown by Le Corbusier's comparative analysis. It *invites*, in Corbu's case, *demands*, the expression of distinct functions through specific and separate elements of the composition. *Structure* and *enclosure* are no longer provided by the single element of wall punctured by carefully dimensioned openings, but by frame and skin, respectively. Perhaps it was at this moment in architectural evolution that the metaphorical idea of 'envelope' became possible, when the internal volumes of a building could be enclosed by, to return to our dictionary definition, a 'covering' or a 'wrapper'.

The other development in building technique with a significant bearing on this discussion was the emergence of the apparatus of mechanical systems of environmental control.[9] This had a number of important consequences. It made it possible to achieve a greater distinction between external and internal climates than the fabric, aided only by primitive heat and light sources, could offer. It made it possible to conceive of buildings, for an ever-increasing range of specialised uses, to be inhabited for 24 hours a day and for 365 days a year. Most importantly, it allowed the environmental function of the envelope to be replaced by the input of machines. In Ludwig Mies van der Rohe's glass skyscraper projects (Figure 7.4), the envelope was

7.4 Ludwig Mies van der Rohe, glass skyscraper project, Berlin, Germany (1919).

almost entirely dematerialised and, even though these visionary designs would almost certainly have been uninhabitable if built when they were first conceived, their progeny became the most ubiquitous building type of the twentieth century. In these built examples, located in all climates, the primary environmental function of the building enclosure played a relatively minor role in their environmental strategy (Figure 7.5).

Coming to the present day, the picture is much more complex than the clear-cut certainties of either the Renaissance or of post-Miesian Modernism. New developments in the techniques of building have greatly expanded the tectonic and environmental repertoire and the proper concern for the agenda of sustainability has redefined the objectives of environmental design. As a consequence, the design of the building envelope is potentially more challenging than ever before.

In the early history of environmental control in architecture, the building envelope was the principal agent of climate modification. Then, the development of mechanical systems transferred the environmental function from envelope to plant. Now, the focus has shifted towards developing a deeper understanding of the potential of the envelope as a key element of the environmental system and in establishing new relationships between envelope and plant.

The buildings described and analysed in the Case Studies that follow serve to illustrate this aspect of 'selective' design. They are drawn from many continents (Figure 7.6) and include examples of the principal non-domestic building types. The aim was to show that the principles of 'selective' design characterised much of the best of contemporary practice. In each case, the primary climatic conditions are summarised and the principal parameters of the comfort requirements of the building outlined while the primary environmental strategy is described.

7.6 Locations of Case Studies: 1, Al Khobar, Saudi Arabia; 2, Milton Keynes, UK; 3, Kempsey, New South Wales, Australia; 4, Victoria, British Columbia, Canada; 5, Gebze, Turkey; 6, Nouméa, New Caledonia; 7, Harare, Zimbabwe; 8, Yountville, California, USA; 9, Ahmedabad, India.

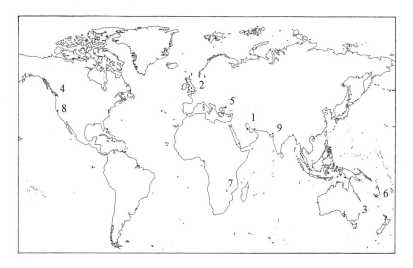

Case Study 1

APICORP Headquarters Building, Al Khobar, Saudi Arabia

ARCHITECT: DEGW

This building is the headquarters of the international Arab Petroleum Investments Corporation (APICORP). It accommodates office processes similar to those found in corporate headquarters around the globe and means that the environmental specification is, in its general nature, similar to that of any building of this type, wherever it is located. When set against the extreme climate of the region, however, this makes the environmental design challenge particularly demanding. For six months of the year the ambient temperature is > 40°C and relative humidity is often > 90%. The solar altitude at this latitude leads to high levels of incident radiation on the ground and on the roof surface of any building.

1.1 Sunpath diagram for latitude 26.5°N.

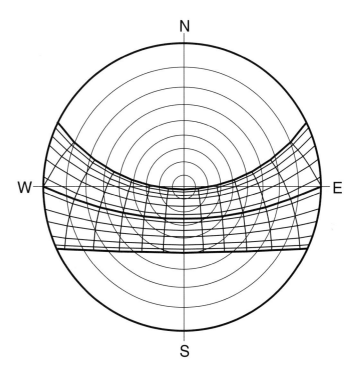

1.2 Temperature (°C).

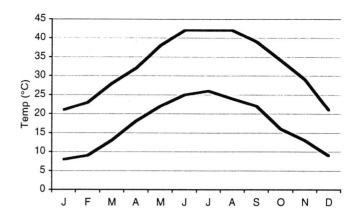

1.3 Relative humidity (%).

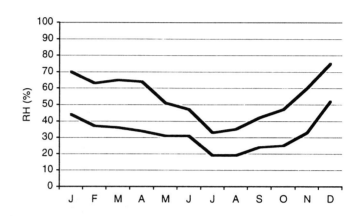

1.4 Precipitation (mm).

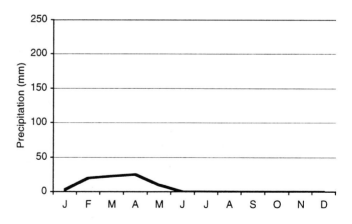

The form of the building derives most fundamentally from analysis of the environmental problem. The oversailing concrete vaulted roof provides primary protection from the glare of the sun. Beneath the roof is a clear hierarchy of space. The service elements, staircases, lavatories, kitchens, and so forth, which are less demanding environmentally than the working areas, occupy the edge and thus act as a defensive line between the external environment and the controlled conditions within. The office space is organised on two asymmetrical floor plates, each of three storeys, either side of a central atrium. Each floor plate is penetrated by two courtyards, which admit controlled natural light and assist in the ventilation processes of the building. The primary structure of the building is of concrete. The roof vaults are double-skinned allowing the void to serve as a return air plenum for the air-conditioning plant, which is necessary in this extreme climate.

1.5 Ground floor plan. *Source:* Slessor 1998.

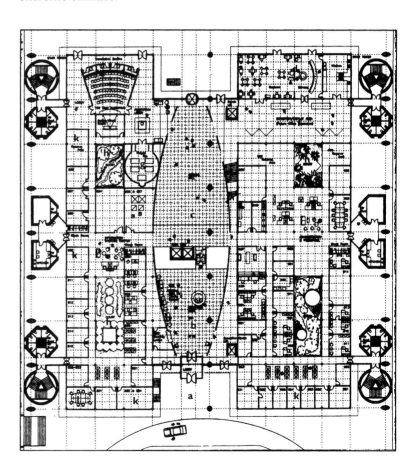

The principle of selective environmental design rests upon the use of the form and materiality of a building to provide the primary response in bridging the gap between the external and internal environments. This building, with its explicit and hierarchical expression of its individual elements, is a demonstration of this approach. It sits clearly in the lineage of the twentieth-century office building that perhaps began with Frank Lloyd Wright's Larkin Building in Buffalo of 1903 and led to the ubiquitous atrium buildings of the 1980s and 1990s. The clear

1.6 Typical office-level plan. *Source:* Slessor 1998.

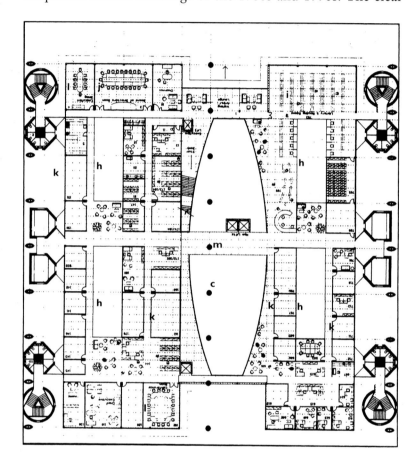

1.7 Cross-section.

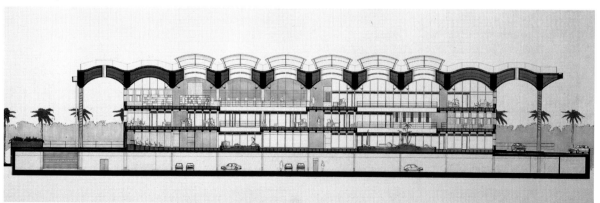

logic that informs the design suggests that its principles could be applied as a 'type' solution to the problem of the office building, and possibly other building functions, in hot–arid locations. The design unambiguously makes use of the scientific knowledge and technical expertise that plays such a central role in modern civilisation, but it also evinces a regard for what Kenneth Frampton, in his argument for a 'Critical Regionalism', described as 'the contingencies of climate and the temporally inflected qualities of local light'.

1.8 Exterior. *Source:* Slessor 1998.

1.9 Interior. *Source:* Slessor 1998.

References

Francis Duffy *et al.*, *Design for Change: The Architecture of DEGW*, Watermark, Haslemere and Birkhauser, Basel, 1998.

Kenneth Frampton, 'Towards a critical regionalism: six points for an architecture of resistance', in Hal Foster (ed.), *Postmodern Culture*, Pluto, London and Concord, MA, 1983.

Catherine Slessor, 'Sheltering sky', *Architectural Review*, March 1998, pp. 34–9.

Case Study 2

The Berrill Building, Open University, Milton Keynes, UK

ARCHITECT: FEILDEN CLEGG

The Open University (OU) was founded in 1969 to extend opportunities for university education to students outside the conventional education system. It has grown to become the biggest university in the world, with 450,000 students, all of whom are served by its central campus in the new city of Milton Keynes in Buckinghamshire. However, the OU is unlike almost all other universities in that its students work through the medium of what is now referred to as 'distance learning'. The campus is, therefore, primarily the location for academic staff and administration. The Berrill Building is, in essence, an office building that houses a number of university departments and the principal visitors' reception to the campus.

2.1 Sunpath diagram for latitude 52°N.

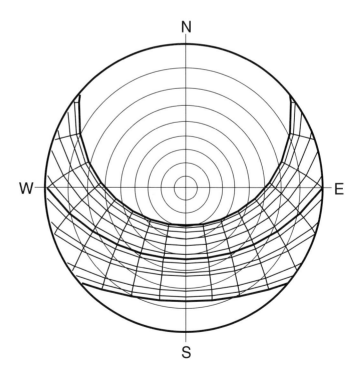

2.2 Temperature (°C).

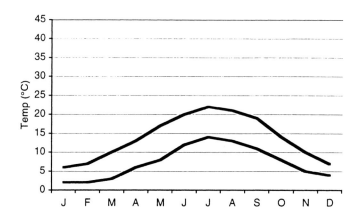

2.3 Relative humidity (%).

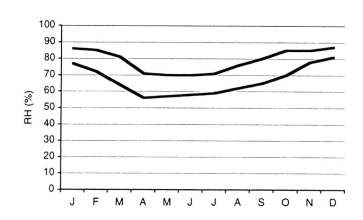

2.4 Precipitation (mm).

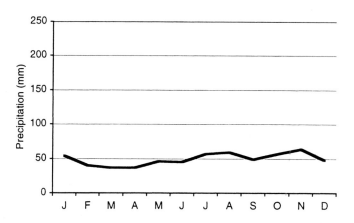

2.5 Plan at entrance level.

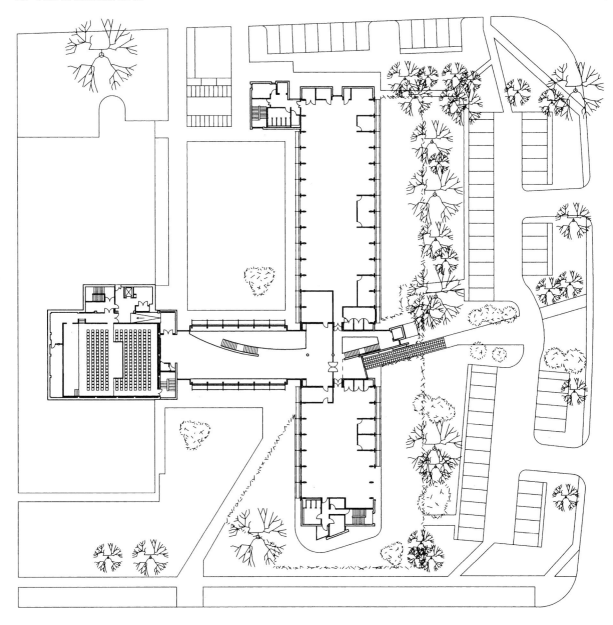

At first sight, the building is a simple five-storey office slab with its long axis oriented north–south. However, this apparent simplicity conceals a sophisticated understanding of the means by which effective environmental control may be achieved for contemporary office work. The strategy is to integrate the form, materials and mechanical systems to create a high-quality working environment with low-energy consumption, working within the constraints of a modest budget.

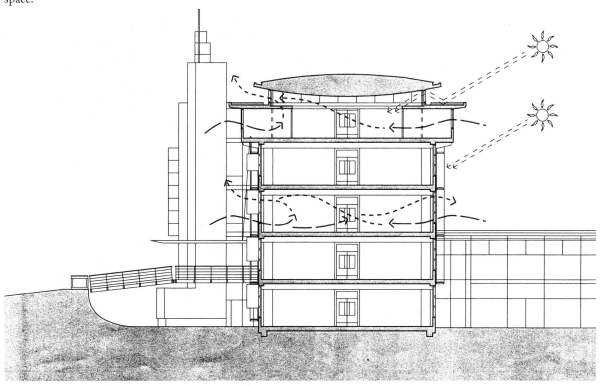

The first step was to establish the overall form. The building is 14 metres deep, which allows good levels of natural lighting and permits simple cross-ventilation. The orientation was determined more by the characteristics of the site than by environmental concerns. This exposes the building to low-angle sunlight, which can cause glare and, particularly on a western façade in the summer months in the UK, a risk of overheating. To achieve good levels of daylight the façades are relatively highly glazed and the risk of glare and solar-gain is mitigated by the design of sophisticated external solar shading. This is subtly different in response to the different conditions of each orientation. To the east, fixed, perforated aluminium panels are suspended perpendicular to the façade to admit early sunlight but to provide shade as the day progresses. On the more exposed west façade is a system of photocell-controlled roller blinds that protect against low-angle solar gains in the afternoons.

The structure of the building is of *in-situ* reinforced concrete. This is exposed internally in columns, beams and ceilings to provide the thermal mass that controls temperature fluctuations. In addition, the geometry of the structure is manipulated in the interests of the environmental strategy of the building. The load-bearing columns are at 3 metre centres and support deep, exposed beams, which span the full 14-metre width of the building. The

columns are slender and blade-like in plan, which allows them to reflect daylight into the office space and to soften the contrast in brightness between the interior and the sky.

The building is conceived as a system of interconnected elements and processes served by a district heating system, which supplies its simple hot water radiators. These are zoned east and west on each floor to allow an effective response to solar gains, fitted as they are with thermostatic radiator valves. Ventilation is achieved by occupant-controlled low-level opening lights in the curtain-wall system and by high-level vents, which are automatically activated by temperature sensors in summer, but are inoperable when the heating system is in use. This helps to avoid unnecessary ventilation heat loss in winter. The natural and artificial lighting is integrated through sensors that monitor whether the space is occupied and the level of available daylight.

The shallow-plan office building is one of the most familiar of all modern building types. Throughout its history, it has undergone a sequence of transformations as developments have occurred in the technologies of structure, construction and mechanical services. In the 1960s, the combination of the adoption of frame construction, lightweight internal partitioning, open-plan and the highly glazed curtain-wall produced a marked transformation in its environmental performance. In temperate climates, these buildings suffered from extreme summer overheating and greatly increased heat loss and thermal discomfort in winter. It was almost as if they had been transported to a different climate. This led to a shift towards deeper plan and highly serviced buildings, to the emergence of 'exclusive' environmental control. The significance of the Berrill Building is that it has restored the utility of the shallow plan by demonstrating that, through careful and inventive design of the structure and envelope, it can meet all of the environmental demands of the modern office function.

2.9 Interior. © Dennis Gilbert, View.

Reference

'Building study: design for learning', *Architects' Journal*, 2 April 1998, pp. 33–42.

Case Study 3

Local History Museum and Tourist Office, Kempsey, New South Wales, Australia

ARCHITECT: GLENN MURCUTT

The buildings that Glenn Murcutt has made in Australia in the last 30 years are one of the most convincing demonstrations of the way in which the demands of climate and environment can be translated into architecture of the utmost eloquence. In a sequence of small buildings, the majority single-family houses, he has shown that the universal tenets of the Modern Movement can be adapted to specific conditions of site and climate to become truly regionalist. His design sketches, such as those for the Landscape Interpretation Centre at Kakadu in the Northern Territory of Australia, reveal the precise relationship he establishes between solar geometry and the built form as a fundamental influence upon the formation of his architecture.

The Local History Museum and Tourist Office at Kempsey was built in two phases between 1976 and 1988. The climate on the coast of New South Wales to the north of Sydney is warm in winter and very hot in summer. The heat is tempered by cooling north-easterly breezes from the sea.

3.1 Sunpath diagram for latitude 31°S.

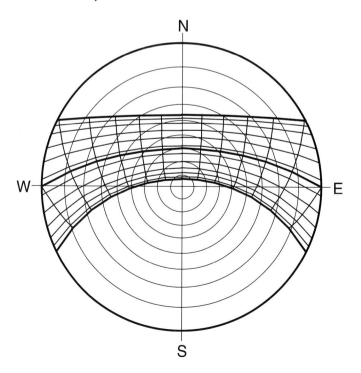

3.2 Temperature (°C).

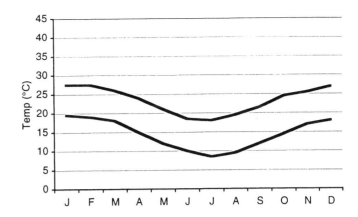

3.3 Relative humidity (%).

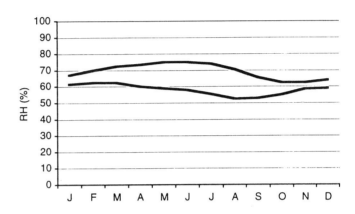

3.4 Precipitation (mm).

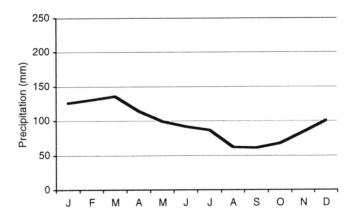

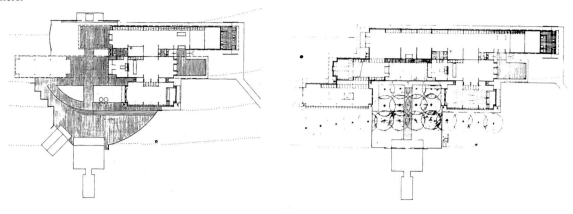

3.5 Plans. *Source:* John McAslan & Partners.

The fundamental element of the building is a simple, steel-framed pavilion form whose curved roof permits clerestorey lighting and natural ventilation through industrial ventilators positioned at the apex of the curve. The plan is an arrangement of three parallel pavilions with the entrance to the building positioned in the central one. The building was constructed in two stages. In the first phase, the plan was relatively compact, but the extension in the second phase has made it more open with the creation of a central veranda and courtyard, the fourth side of which is a reconstructed cottage, a key exhibit of the museum. The clerestorey windows, which are the principal light source, take two forms. The standard condition is that they are a continuation of the roof plane and shaded by external, slatted sunscreens. On the south façade they are steeply inclined above the metal-clad wall and have internal louvered shades.

3.6 Transverse cross-section. *Source:* John McAslan & Partners.

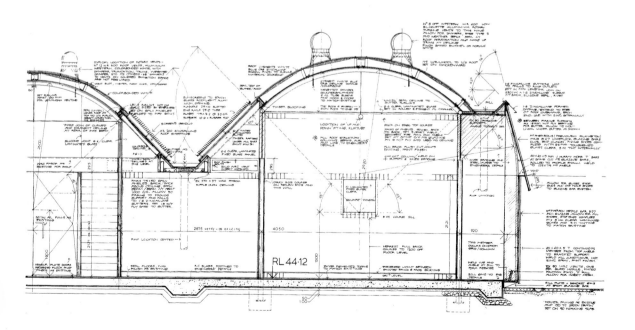

3.7 Exterior. *Source:* Max Dupain & Associates.

3.8 Detail of the entrance. *Source:* Max Dupain & Associates.

The language of the building clearly expresses and differentiates the elements of its construction. The roof is of lightweight corrugated steel with thermal insulation between the outer and inner skins. The external walls are zinc clad and cedar lattice screens shelter external verandas. Internal partitions are non-load-bearing brickwork and the concrete floor slab is exposed. These provide the building with a degree of thermal mass with which to moderate the thermal environment.

Murcutt's buildings belie their apparent modesty in the manner in which they are so precisely adapted to the conditions of climate, construction and culture that arise from their locations and programmes. They show how architecture of universal significance may arise from a proper understanding and interpretation of these specific facts.

3.9 Interior with the layout of exhibits. *Source:* Max Dupain & Associates.

References

Françoise Fromonot, *Glenn Murcutt: Buildings and Projects*, Whitney Library of Design and Watson-Guptill, New York, 1995.

Case Study 4

Strawberry Vale School, Victoria, British Columbia, Canada

Architect: Patkau Architects

Designs for school buildings have played a significant role in the relatively brief history of energy-conscious architectural design. St George's School at Wallasey built, in 1958, in the North West of England, with its vast solar wall, was raised to iconic status by Rayner Banham in *The Architecture of the Well-tempered Environment* (1969). In recent years the theme has been taken forward by other designs, such as Sergio Los's Crossara School in Northern Italy and the work of Hampshire County Council in the UK. Pragmatically, the fact that school buildings are mainly occupied during daylight hours makes them particularly well suited to exploit solar gains for space heating in the winter months at high latitudes. There is also a symbolic appropriateness in the association of naturally sustained environments with the needs of children. Patkau Architects' design for the Strawberry Vale School at Victoria, British Columbia, sits securely in this tradition and develops the conventions and principles of the low-energy school in a rich and eloquent architectural language.

4.1 Sunpath diagram for latitude 49°N.

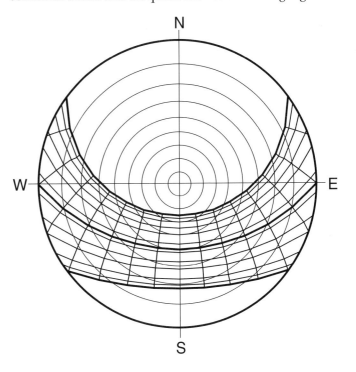

4.2 Temperature (°C).

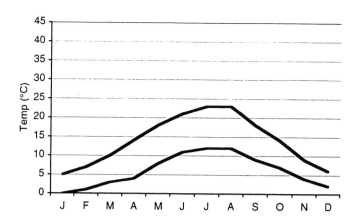

4.3 Relative humidity (%).

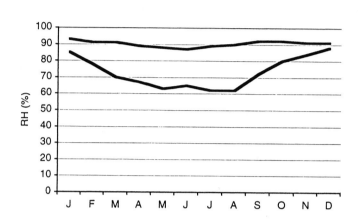

4.4 Precipitation (mm).

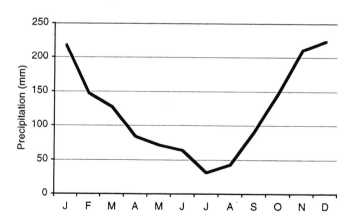

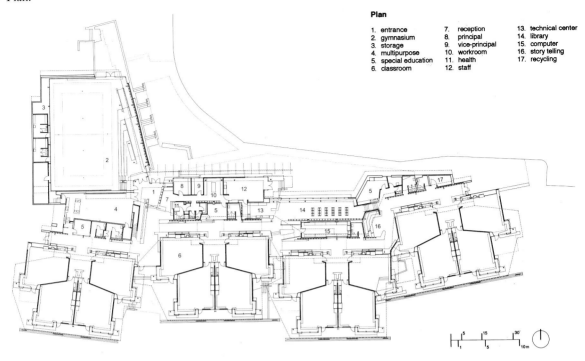

Plan

1.	entrance	7.	reception	13.	technical center
2.	gymnasium	8.	principal	14.	library
3.	storage	9.	vice-principal	15.	computer
4.	multipurpose	10.	workroom	16.	story telling
5.	special education	11.	health	17.	recycling
6.	classroom	12.	staff		

The plan observes the rule of southerly orientation for the main classroom spaces, which, at northerly latitudes, allows low-angle winter sun to bring warmth and light and makes it relatively easy to avoid unwanted solar gains in the summer with fixed shading devices. The interlocking plan form of the groups of four classrooms allows each room to enjoy the benefits of the orientation through their corner windows and achieves a measure of compactness to control heat losses in the cold Canadian winter. In section, the floor levels follow the natural contours of the site and the roof plane is manipulated to control the volume to be heated, provide daylight through carefully designed rooflights and to promote natural ventilation by a stack-effect. The heating system and the artificial lighting have been designed to optimise the benefits of solar heat gains and natural light.

The environmental strategy of the building is expressed in the meticulous coding of the structure and materiality of the building. Steel is used only for those primary structural members that would be uneconomical in first-growth timber, but all else is in is clearly expressed timber. Externally, the transition from enclosed, heated space to overhang is indicated by a change in the plane and profile of the roof cladding. The mechanical systems are exposed within the building, which makes them easy to maintain, and they express something of the functional

4.6 Cross-sections.

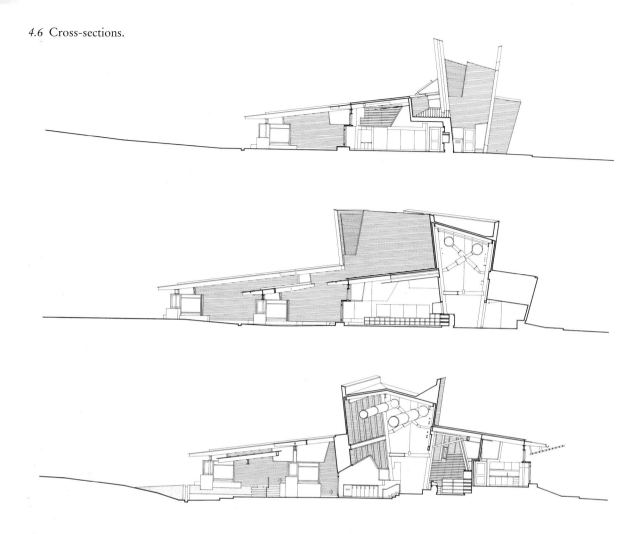

4.7 Exterior from the east. *Source:* Patkau Architects.

relationship between the envelope and the plant in the process of environmental control. The internal walls and partitions are finished in either timber boarding or plywood.

Similar themes continue in the design of the external landscape. The intention is positively to exploit the presence of the building to sustain rather than damage its setting. Rainwater collected from the roof is channelled into a linear watercourse on the north side of the building where it is hoped aquatic plants will be propagated by natural migration. All of the site water is collected in a shallow marsh, where microbial processes filter it before it re-enters the ground.

All of this attention to detail results in an architecture of great subtlety and richness. In pioneering designs, such as St George's School, the environmental agenda was mechanically expressed through the great solar wall and the characteristic cross-section sloping from south to north. The issues were writ large in the

4.8 Interior central space. *Source:* Patkau Architects.

language and little attention was given to specificity or fine detail. At Strawberry Vale, the language has become much more complex. Developments in the understanding of environmental processes now allow a more refined response to the nature of the environment, which is more diverse, spatially and temporally, and to its translation into architectural form.

4.9 Detail of a classroom corner.
Source: Patkau Architects.

Reference
'Strawberry Vale School British Columbia', *Domus*, no. 789, 1997.

Case Study 5

Yapi Kredi Operations Centre, Gebze, Turkey

ARCHITECT: JOHN MCASLAN AND PARTNERS

This building, which is on a south-facing hillside sloping towards the Sea of Marmara, accommodates the Yapi Kredi Bank's day-to-day administrative operations, including its computer centre, document processing and staff training. This means that the internal environment must be suitable for the performance of the functions of the modern international corporation.

The design is based upon the strong geometrical diagram of a tartan-grid in which standard, square-plan office pavilions are interconnected by a network of covered streets. This allows the building to follow the steep contours of the site and to acknowledge the seismic problems of the region. It also permits the development of a sophisticated response to the environmental questions posed by the climate.

5.1 Sunpath diagram for latitude 41°N.

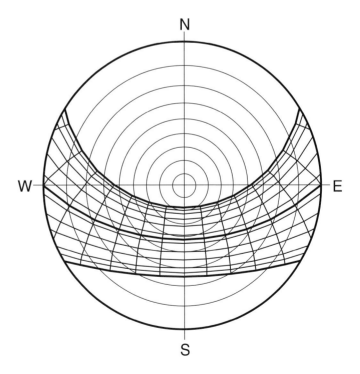

5.2 Temperature (°C).

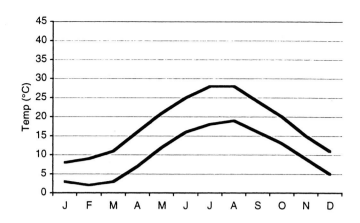

5.3 Relative humidity (%).

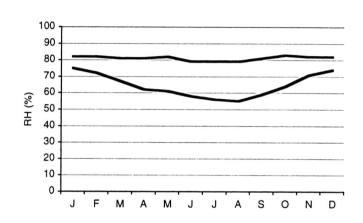

5.4 Precipitation (mm).

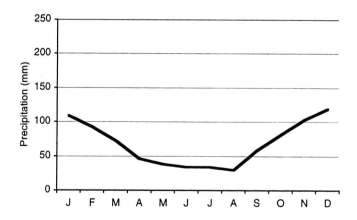

The streets are designed as intermediate environments for circulation, eating places and informal meetings. They also serve to buffer the office pavilions from the extremes of the external climate. Their roofs are formed by taut fabric canopies, supported on steel structural frames with strips of clear glazing at the junction where they connect with the pavilions. This arrangement provides a high degree of protection to the highly glazed façades of the offices, shading them from direct sunlight. Retractable blinds provide a second line of defence. The exposed external façades have a system of fixed shading devices to the east, south and west, and the internal courtyards bring additional daylight to the centre of each pavilion.

5.5 Plans showing the relationships between pavilions and the internal streets (from *Architectural Review*, March 1998).

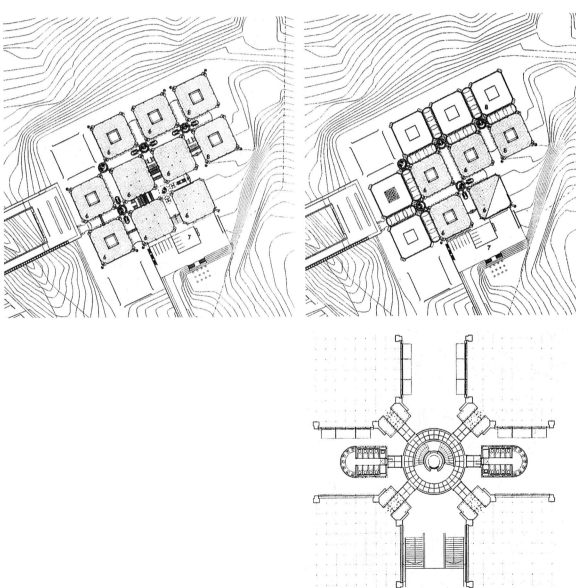

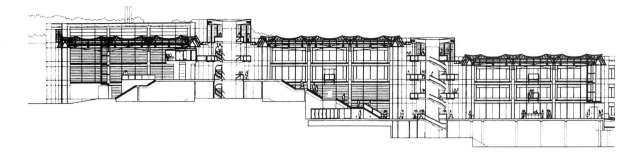

5.6 Longitudinal cross-section from the north-east to the south-west. (from *Architectural Review*, March 1998)

The strategy provides a hierarchy of environmental conditions that range from the precise control of the office spaces to the more dynamic quality of the streets. In these, waste heat from the air-conditioned offices is used, when necessary, to ensure they are comfortable for the more relaxed uses that take place in them.

The strict discipline of the orthogonal tartan-grid signals the allegiance of the design to the rational tradition of twentieth-century architecture. In a process of architectural evolution, the building further develops the potential of this language through the superimposition of new layers of environmental control.

5.7 South external entrance. © Peter Cook, View.

Reference
Fred Harvey, 'Street credit', *Architectural Review*, March 1998, pp. 18–26.

Case Study 6

Tjibaou Cultural Centre, Nouméa, New Caledonia

ARCHITECT: RENZO PIANO

Renzo Piano is one of the major figures in the world of contemporary architecture. Since he and Richard Rogers won the competition for the design of the Centre Georges Pompidou in Paris over 30 years ago his work has undergone a remarkable transformation. Since the almost overwhelming expression of the capabilities of mechanical processes of environmental control at Pompidou, perhaps the ultimate 'exclusive' mode building, Piano has progressively confronted the issues of environmental design and has consistently offered new insights into the definition of the environmental agenda. Kenneth Frampton has pointed to Piano's relationship with the principles of Baconian empirical science, and it is this belief in the potential of objective analysis as the basis of architectural invention that has invested his designs with their originality and avoidance of the dictates of passing fashion.

6.1 Sunpath diagram for latitude 22.5°N.

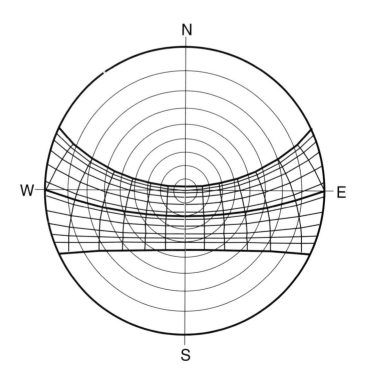

6.2 Temperature (°C).

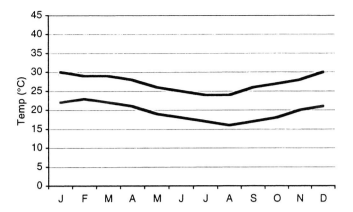

6.3 Relative humidity (%).

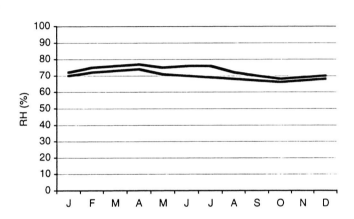

6.4 Precipitation (mm).

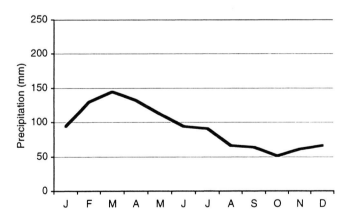

The aim of the Tjibaou Cultural Centre in New Caledonia in the Western Pacific is to celebrate and preserve the culture of the Kanak people. The programme for the building required spaces to house permanent exhibitions of artefacts and to accommodate live enactment of dance and similar events. The design is possibly the most remarkable example of Piano's application of fundamental physical principles in the production of original architectural form. The plan takes the form of a gently curved passage, which runs along the axis of a small peninsula. Arrayed along this are three 'villages' that house distinct functions; Village 1: interpretation, galleries and performance; Village 2: resource centre, libraries and multimedia; and Village 3: youth centre and school. Each village utilises a generic cross-section in which relatively low-ceilinged, orthogonal spaces are connected to tall, curved forms, referred to by Piano as 'cases'. These are fabricated from aluminium and the indigenous hardwood, iroko.

Piano has written of the relationship between his design and the forms of the traditional Kanak village. The tall huts of the vernacular promote efficient natural ventilation by the stack-effect and this principle is adopted in the design of the new buildings. In the modern building, however, the tools of architectural science – computer simulation and scale-model studies in a wind tunnel – have been used to refine the design. The *cases* drive a flow of natural ventilation across the section through the relatively conventional low volumes. This is controlled by a

6.5 Conceptual sketch. *Source:*
Rienzo Piano Building Workshop.

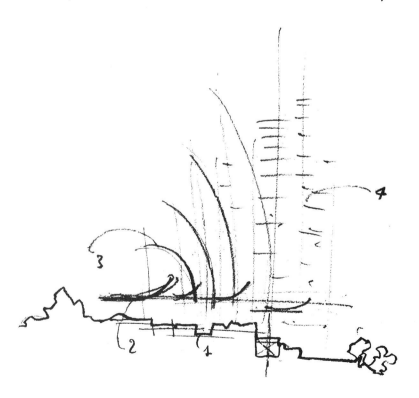

6.6 Site plan. *Source:* Rienzo Piano
Building Workshop.

6.7 Floor plan. *Source:* Rienzo Piano
Building Workshop.

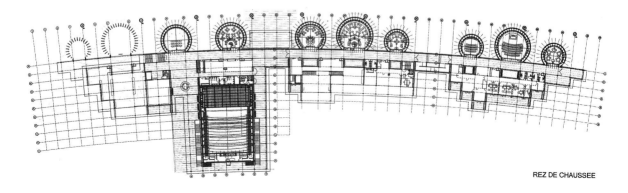

system of adjustable louvres that allow the building to respond to changes in the direction and velocity of the wind. The low roofs are double-skinned to provide protection against the heat of the high sun.

The project is clearly a very special case in which the symbolic is as significant as the technical. Piano's aim was to make a distinction between culture and technique, to separate the skills that have been acquired over the years in his Building Workshop from the European culture from which they have been born. That is to reject the culture of, in his own words, 'Leonardo da Vinci and Freud, Kant and Darwin, Louis XIV and Don Quixote', and to attempt to 'create a symbol: a cultural centre devoted to Kanak civilisation, the place that would represent them to foreigners and that would pass on their memory to

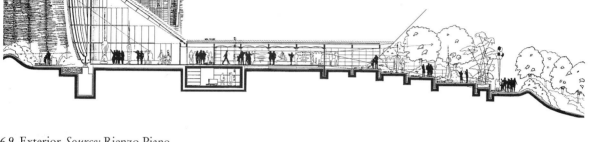

6.8 Cross-section of Village 1. *Source:* Rienzo Piano Building Workshop.

6.9 Exterior. *Source:* Rienzo Piano Building Workshop, © Gollings.

their grandchildren'. In most circumstances the act of generating form from a combination of vernacular reference and the analytical procedures of architectural science would seem simplistic, too literal and mechanistic an application of Ricoeur's distinction between regional culture and international civilisation. In the unique conditions at Tjibaou, where the need was for the specific not the generic, the outcome seems particularly apt.

6.10 Salle de Spectacle. *Source:* Rienzo Piano Building Workshop, © W Vassal.

References

Sheila McInstry, 'Sea and sky', *Architectural Review*, December 1998, pp. 30–7.

Renzo Piano, *The Renzo Piano Logbook*, Preface by Kenneth Frampton, Thames & Hudson, London, 1997.

Ricoeur cited in Kenneth Frampton, 'Towards a critical regionalism', op. cit.

Case Study 7

Eastgate Office Building, Harare, Zimbabwe

ARCHITECT: PEARCE PARTNERSHIP

This building is a significant event in the recent development of environmentally responsive architecture in Africa. It abandons the universal formula of the curtain-walled, air-conditioned office building and, in its place, works with the principles of thermal mass and natural ventilation to provide a comfortable working environment in this demanding climate.

The climate of Harare, which is at an altitude of 1500 metres, has eight months of the year when it is dry with hot days and cool nights and four months when it is hot and humid. The aim of the design was to achieve comfort around the year without reliance upon expensive, imported components, such as air-conditioning plant, and with consequential savings in operating costs. In these respects, the building is an exemplar of the way in which inventive design may provide solutions that are both technologically and culturally appropriate for the emerging economies.

7.1 Sunpath diagram for latitude 18°S.

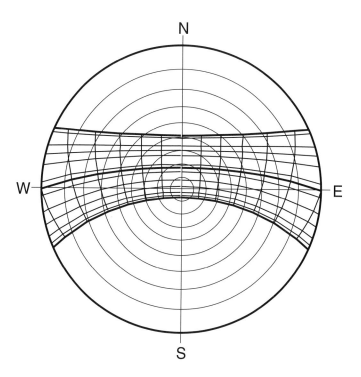

7.2 Temperature (°C).

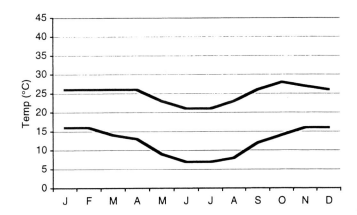

7.3 Relative humidity (%).

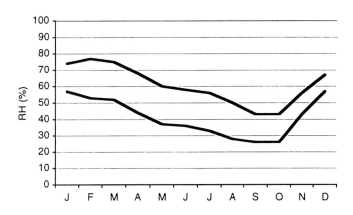

7.4 Precipitation (mm).

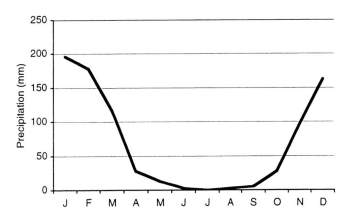

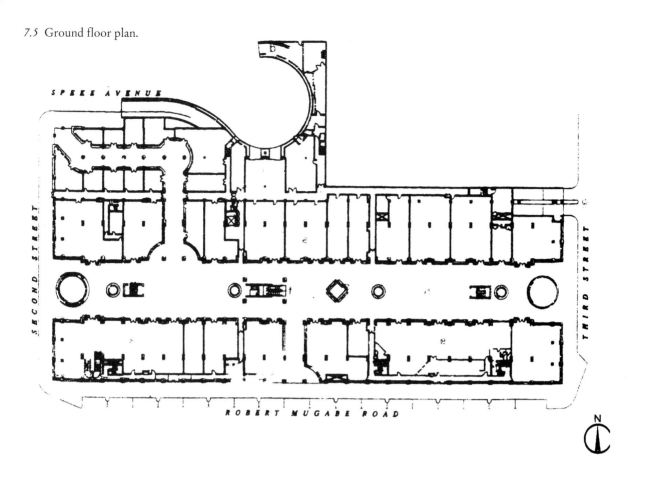

SPEKE AVENUE

SECOND STREET

THIRD STREET

ROBERT MUGABE ROAD

N

The plan is a simple arrangement of two parallel, nine-storey office wings, each 15 metres deep, separated by a full-height atrium, which is also 15 metres wide. The structure of the building is of massive *in-situ* concrete with concrete and brick cladding. Wherever possible the mass is exposed. The structure is extended at each floor level to form balconies, which shade the walls and windows. The windows are limited in size, particularly on the north façade where they are < 25% of the surface area. All windows have filters to control glare and are sealed. The building is ventilated through a network of 32 vertical ducts located in the core of each floor plate. These serve a floor plenum, which delivers air to the office spaces through grilles under the windows. The concrete floor, which remains at ~20°C throughout the year, provides cooling to the air in the hot periods of the year and a degree of heating in the cool season. Auxiliary heaters are located in the spaces to supply further warmth when needed. The air is extracted through high-level bulkheads into large vertical shafts that rise above the roof and become expressed as a powerful element of the architecture.

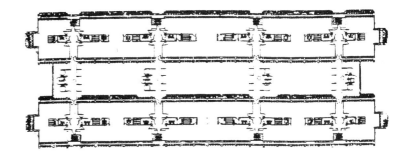

7.6 Typical office floor plan (upper level).

7.7 Cross-section showing the principles of general energy management.

In adopting the principles of structural cooling and natural ventilation, the design cannot deliver the precision of temperature control that conventional air-conditioning can achieve. The aim has been to keep the maximum temperature within a wider definition of comfort, in the range 21–25°C. This has been accepted by the office workers and is a practical demonstration of the application of the emerging theories of environmental comfort (see Chapter 4).

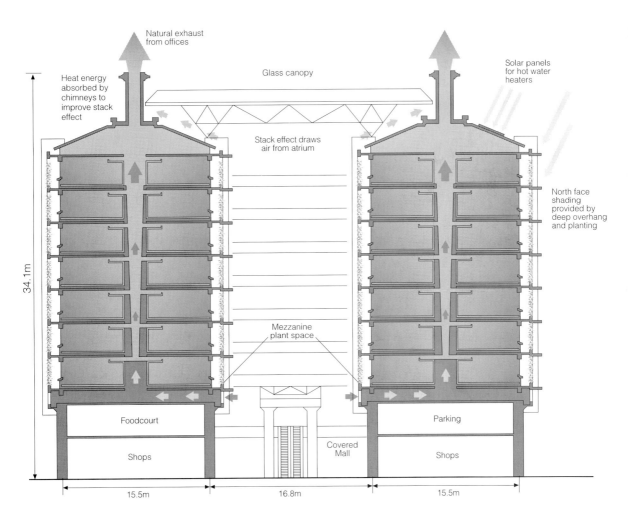

7.8 *(facing page)* Exterior.
7.9 Exterior façade detail.

This building is the largest mixed-development project yet constructed in Zimbabwe and demonstrates the commitment of its promoters to find new solutions to the design of this essential element of the fabric of the modern commercial city appropriate for the economic and cultural circumstances of developing African nations. It is a skilful adaptation of the stereotype of the atrium office building to the conditions of the tropical climate.

7.10 Atrium.

Reference
'Building Feature: Eastgate', *CAArchitect News Net*, no. 4, 1997, pp. 6–7.

Case Study 8

Winery, Napanook Vineyard, Yountville, California, USA

Architects: Herzog and de Meuron

Modern wine production involves a high degree of process control. The fermentation tanks, which are at the heart of the process, are now highly insulated and fitted with very precise means of regulating their temperature. The Napa Valley, which lies north of San Francisco, is the heart of the Californian wine region and Herzog and de Meuron's design for the new winery at the Napanook Vineyard is a remarkable combination of sophisticated modern technology and age-old principles of environmental control.

In its fundamentals the building is a simple two-storey pavilion, 140 metres long and 25 metres deep. Its long axis runs almost north–south and it is penetrated by two tall, wide openings which form the entrance and the loading bay. With the exception of the relatively small administrative area, which is on the first floor at the northern end of the plan, the building has virtually no mechanical environmental services. The enclosing envelope, which wraps around the simple steel structural frame,

8.1 Sunpath diagram for latitude 38°N.

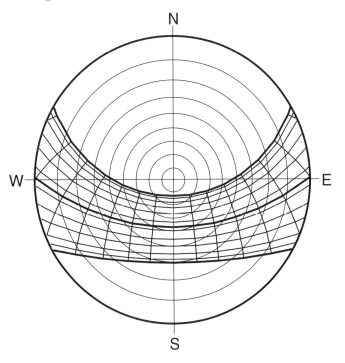

8.2 Temperature (°C).

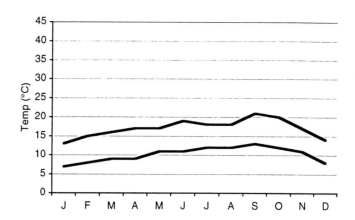

8.3 Relative humidity (%).

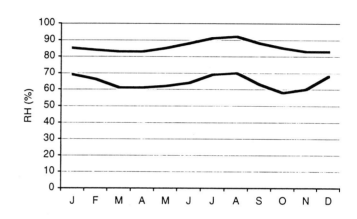

8.4 Precipitation (mm).

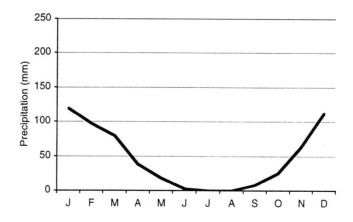

8.5 Ground-floor plan.

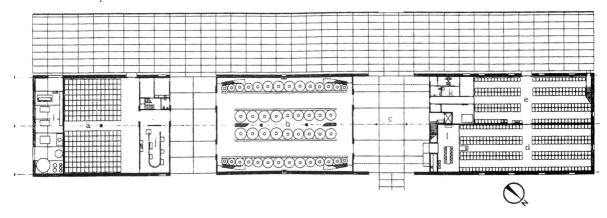

8.6 First-floor plan.

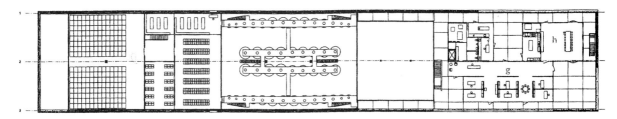

8.7 Cross-section through the cellars.

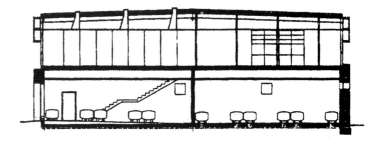

8.8 Cross-section through the tank room.

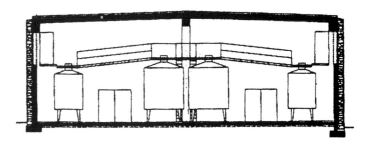

is made from galvanised steel gabions, wire cages of dimensions 900 × 450 × 450 millimetres, filled with crushed basalt. Stacked up and supported from the structural frame, these become a rainscreen cladding and give the building a high level of thermal mass. Within this simple system, the performance of the envelope is precisely calibrated to meet the varying environmental demands of the process within. By using three sizes of mesh and three grades of stone, it is possible to vary the density and transparency of the enclosure.

The fermentation process in the tank room at the heart of the plan can tolerate some degree of environmental variation and its enclosure, plus that of the covered outdoor spaces, is enclosed in the coarsest grade of stone. This allows sunlight to filter in and permits cross-ventilation through the interstices of the stone and apertures in the internal glazed screen. The cask cellars and the warehouse, which are at the north and south ends of the plan, need greater temperature control and their

8.9 Exterior. © Margherita Spiluttini.

envelope is made of the finer grade stone, which is opaque to the transmission of light. In the cask cellars, the floor is made of crushed basalt upon which the oak wine casks stand on concrete sleepers. This arrangement allows humidity from the ground to permeate the space as an essential part of the wine-maturing process. The thermal mass of the enclosure is maintained by using crushed basalt as a topping over the flat roof structure.

The building is elegant in both conception and execution. The key to the design is the definition of distinct zones of environmental control, from the loose-fit of the tank room to the more precise control of the administrative areas. This analysis determines the density and thermal mass of the cladding and the relation of solid to void. The result shows how a deep understanding of the physical principles of environmental control, when allied with a capacity for invention, can produce an architecture that is both original and appropriate to its purpose and context.

8.10 Interior. © Margherita Spiluttini.

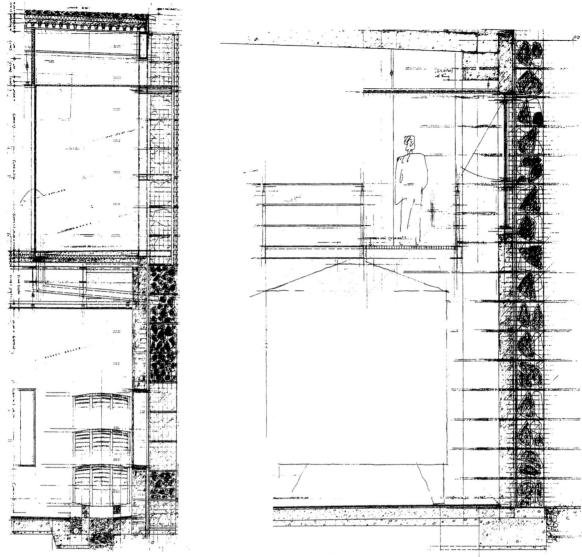

detailed wall section through office and cellar   **detailed wall section through tank room**

typical horizontal wall section

Reference

Annette Lecuyer, 'Steel, stone and sky', *Architectural Review*, October 1998, pp. 44–8.

Case Study 9

Torrent Pharmaceuticals Research Laboratory, Ahmedabad, India

ARCHITECTS: ABHIKRAM ARCHITECTS, AHMEDABAD, AND BRIAN FORD ASSOCIATES, LONDON

The processes of natural ventilation have been extensively researched as part of the scientific support for the revival of the use of non-mechanical processes of environmental control in buildings. The Torrent Pharmaceuticals building at Ahmedabad is the product of a collaboration between the Indian architects Abhikram and the British architect–environmentalist Brian Ford.

The significance of the building is that it applies the principles of natural cooling, ventilation and lighting, of selective design, to the design of a building type which conventionally relies upon mechanical solutions for environmental control. Furthermore, it achieves this successfully in a climate that, because of the extremely high ambient temperatures experienced, is inherently hostile.

The process adopted is, in effect, a development of the vernacular device of the 'wind-catcher' that has been used for many centuries in the hot–arid climate of the Middle East. Here, the

9.1 Sunpath diagram for latitude 22.5°N.

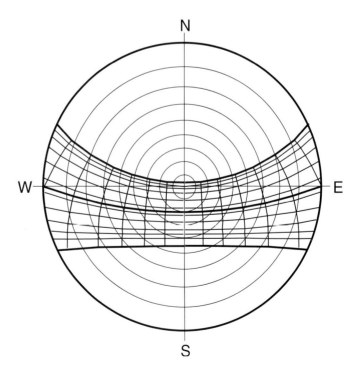

9.2 Temperature (°C).

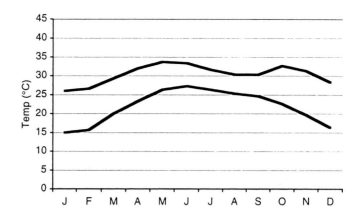

9.3 Relative humidity (%).

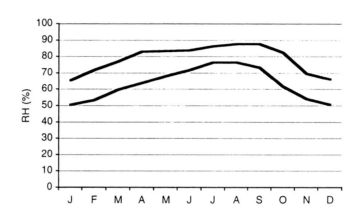

9.4 Precipitation (mm).

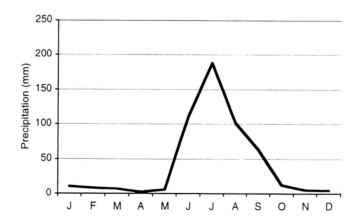

9.5 Site plan.

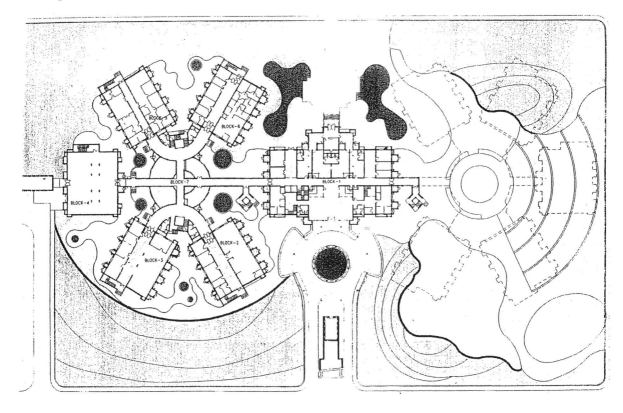

9.6 Cross-section.

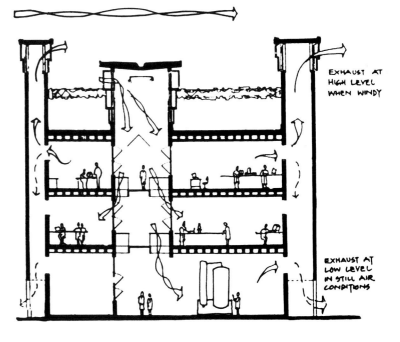

EXHAUST AT
HIGH LEVEL
WHEN WINDY

EXHAUST AT
LOW LEVEL
IN STILL AIR
CONDITIONS

application of modern architectural science has allowed the principles of the wind-catcher to be refined and transformed into a system of 'passive downdraught evaporative cooling' (PDEC). Incoming air is captured by a series of tall towers and is then cooled evaporatively before passing down the central open concourse of the building. From there it enters laboratories and offices at the perimeter. It is finally exhausted through perimeter ducts discharging at high level on windy days or at low level when still air conditions occur. The laboratories and offices have carefully dimensioned and shaded window openings that provide glare-free and solar-controlled natural light. When in use, the building has proved capable of achieving significant reductions of internal air temperature in relation to ambient conditions.

This environmental strategy is explicitly expressed in the form of the building. The tall towers represent the physical processes fundamental to its operation and are also a powerful symbol of its environmental ideology.

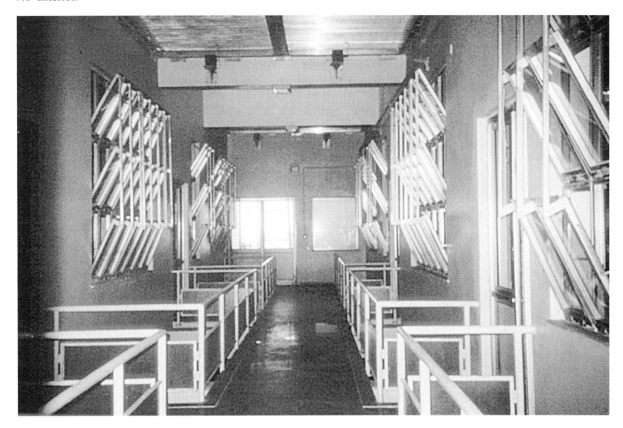

References

Brian Ford, 'Energy and green issues', *Architecture Today*, July 1997.

Susannah Hagan with David Lloyd Jones *et al.*, 'Sustaining an argument: sector analysis – energy efficient buildings', *World Architecture*, March 1999.

Conclusion

All these Case Studies, in their diversity of intention and form, share one common principle: their nature is determined in some fundamental way by the expression of their functional, constructional and material attributes, from their *tectonic* qualities. In the wider theoretical debate, Frampton has argued for the reinstatement of the authority of the tectonic to 'counter the present tendency for architecture to derive its legitimacy from some other discourse'.[10] In other words, to acknowledge the authority of these 'objective' qualities in the complex equation which represents the intention, conception, execution and inhabitation of a building.

This chapter has tried to show that the demands of sustainable design have invested the design of the building envelope with a new discipline. The need to re-establish the function of the envelope as a primary element in the process of environmental control has revived the historic function of the building fabric, but developments in building technique, in structure, construction, material and services, open up rich new possibilities for the language of architecture. Frampton stresses that, in spite of its authority, 'The tectonic does not necessarily favour any particular style.' The richness and variety of the Case Study designs amply reinforce this view. Sound principles of sustainable design are neither formally nor stylistically determinate. It is possible for good architects to apply and adapt them to the specific circumstances of each project – of programme, context, economy and culture. This seems to be right. In these 'post-Post-Modern' times, if we may coin a term, the aim should be to discover the basis of a 'principled diversity'. The issues of sustainability are a key component of those principles.

References

1 Brenda Vale and Robert Vale, *Practical Standard Dictionary*, Funk & Wagnalls, New York, 1928.

2 Rudolf Wittkower, *Architectural Principles in the Age of Humanism*, John Wiley & Sons Ltd, London, 1977.

3 Andrea Palladio, *I quattro libri dell'architettura*, Venice, 1570; English trans. Isaac Ware, *The Four Books of Andrea Palladio's Architecture*, London, 1738; repr. *Andrea Palladio: The Four Books of Architecture*, Introduction by A. K. Placzek, Dover, New York, 1965.

4 Ibid.

5 Mark Girouard, *Robert Smythson and the Elizabethan Country House*, Yale University Press, New Haven, CT, and London, 1983.

6 Dean Hawkes, 'The technical imagination: thoughts in the relation of technique and design', *The Journal of Architecture*, vol. 1, No. 4, Winter 1996, pp. 335–46.

7 Kenneth Frampton (ed. John Cava), *Studies in Tectonic Culture: The Poetics of Construction in Nineteenth and Twentieth Century Architecture*, MIT Press, Cambridge, MA, 1995.

8 Le Corbusier and P. Jeanneret, 'Cinque points d'une architecture nouvelle', *Die Form*, 1926.

9 Rayner Banham, *The Architecture of the Well-Tempered Environment*, Architectural Press, London, 1969.

10 Frampton, *Studies in Tectonic Culture*, op. cit.

8   Environmental design checklist

The architect works with form and mass just as the sculptor does, and like the painter he works with colour. But alone of the three, his is a functional art. It solves practical problems. It creates tools or implements for human beings and utility plays a decisive role in judging it.[1]

In this quotation from Rasmussen, the 'utility' of architecture, discussed here in environmental terms, is determined by the relationship of form and mass to the climatic context. The purpose of this chapter is to suggest the environmental issues to be considered at the various stages of design. It is structured in a way that broadly follows the design process: from overall site considerations, built form and orientation, to detailed environmental aspects of the façade design and, finally, the integration of services. (Orientation is discussed here in terms of 'solar' (south facing in the northern hemisphere, north facing in the southern hemisphere) and 'non-solar' (the converse of 'solar').) However, this in no way presupposes that there is a deterministic or rigid design approach to successful environmentally sensitive architecture. As in the design process, this environmental checklist allows for and encourages the iterative development of ideas and indicates interaction between various stages of design development. Thus, for example, built form may have implications on the level of services, which in turn will influence façade design and the level of user interaction with it. Brief references are made to demonstrate any such interactions.

Central to the philosophy of this design checklist is the aim of minimising environmental impact whilst ensuring comfort conditions. The energy use of buildings is the key to sustainable development (as defined in the Bruntland Report of 1987)[2] and – as is becoming increasingly evident – comfort and well-being,[3] as it relates to global, local and internal environmental conditions. The use of energy in buildings raises concern not only for the consumption in use, but also for the embodied energy in materials. (Embodied energy is not easily quantifiable but can be loosely defined as the amount of energy that has been used to extract and transport raw materials, and to manufacture and transport building components to the site.) This raises detailed issues about the choice of materials in construction.

It is not only these pragmatic aspects that are of interest, but also the enriching of the architectural experience through an understanding and manipulation of environmental characteristics. This broader view is summed up in the term 'selective' architecture.

Selective design

Selective design, as opposed to exclusive design, aims to exploit the climatic conditions to maintain comfort, minimising the need for artificial control reliant on the consumption of energy. This manipulation of climate, to filter selectively positive characteristics of the environment, is achieved through architecture. A building's form is probably the most significant consideration with respect to the selective potential of a design. For example, a building with a large surface-to-volume ratio has the greatest potential to interact with climate, both positively and negatively. Solar gains, daylight and natural ventilation are three aspects where climate can provide useful support to minimise the use of energy for heating, electric lighting and fan power respectively. In recent history, since the advent of fluorescent lighting and air-conditioning, the design emphasis has tended to focus on the negative impact of climate, resulting in minimised interaction with the climate and increased artificial environmental control. Buildings became deep-plan and air-conditioned, with high energy use and low user satisfaction.

The degree to which a building can be selective is dependent on the very first strategic considerations in its design. The environmental design checklist below highlights the issues that can be considered at various stages.

Site analysis

Climate

An initial step in designing in response to the climate is to determine the overall climate type within which the site is located, and to gather relevant climate data, notably temperatures and solar geometry, that are most likely to inform strategic design. The world's climate regions are commonly defined as hot–dry, warm–humid, composite, moderate and cold. Each requires a distinctive climatic design response, as is often embodied in regional primitive architecture and culture.[4]

However, within each climate region a wide variation of climatic characteristics can be found as a result of, for example, altitude, proximity of water mass, urban density, etc. To define a local climate more precisely, further data are required and may include local air temperatures, wind patterns and humidity levels.

The level of detail required for the data is dependent on the likely design role of the climate parameter, and the level of environmental analysis to be performed. For example, a hot–dry climate has relatively large diurnal temperature swings, which can be a significant factor in maintaining comfort though design (e.g. the use of thermal mass). However, in warm–humid climates, the swings are much smaller. It is thus more important to have hourly temperature data for hot–dry climates.

Microclimate

Although the overall climatic context is the primary consideration, microclimatic conditions can be significantly different and therefore will have implications for design. However, it is equally important to consider that a proposed building will influence the microclimate. The microclimate is affected by characteristics of local topography, urbanisation and vegetation.

Topography   The topography of the land will create potential microclimates, which vary from the synoptic conditions. For example, the orientation of a steeply sloping site will affect the amount of solar radiation and hours of sunshine. The orientation of a valley may cause wind funnelling in certain directions and wind sheltering in others (Figure 8.1). Where a landmass meets water, clearly discernible diurnal wind patterns are created. During the day, solar radiation increases the temperature of the land above that of the water, which, through thermal buoyancy of hot air, creates air flow from water to land. At night the effect is reversed.

Urbanisation   The urban microclimate is a topic that has received much attention and clearly demonstrates the importance of assessing the climate in more detail. The most often quoted effect of urbanisation on air temperatures is the 'heat island' effect, where temperatures in cities can be several degrees Celsius higher than neighbouring rural environs.[5] This is caused by a range of factors such as the lack of moisture (fast run-off and little vegetation), the production of heat, the absorption of solar radiation and lower wind speeds in cities (Table 8.1).

8.1 Topography and its effect on diurnal wind patterns. *Source: Achard and Gicquel 1986.*[6]

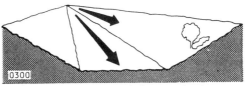

Pre-dawn: *downstream air-flow predominates as cool air washes down the valley.*

Morning: *breeze rises up face of slope due to surface warming.*

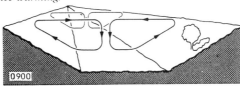

Noon: *air pool in valley has been warmed and creates up-valley breeze.*

Afternoon: *up-valley breeze predominates as surfaces reach maximum temperature.*

Evening: *surfaces cool and start a downward flow of cool air.*

Midnight: *cool heavy air collected in valley begins to flow down stream.*

Table 8.1
Urban microclimate as compared with the rural environs
(Landsberg 1981).

Urban climatic factor	Comparison with rural environs
Temperature (annual mean)	0.5–3.0°C more
Radiation (total horizontal)	0–20% less
Wind speed (annual mean)	20–30% less
Relative humidity (annual mean)	6% less

A more widely appreciated effect of urbanisation is air and noise pollution. Both may have significant consequences on the viability of simple, natural ventilation strategies, and may as a result influence design strategies.

Vegetation The use of planting in improving microclimatic characteristics is well understood. For example, the use of trees as a shelter-belt to protect a site from cold winds is common. However, other benefits for different climate types may include using vegetation to provide evaporative cooling, shading,

8.2 Vegetation provides a variety of microclimates so that people have the opportunity to stand or walk either in the sun or in dappled shade, as in this street in Barcelona, Spain.

filtering of dust particles, some noise attenuation and carbon dioxide absorption, as well as the psychological advantages for man and the ecological benefits of encouraging flora and fauna (Figure 8.2).

Sunpath

The path of the sun is a critical driving force in determining a selective building form, its orientation and façade design. Absorption of solar radiation through the building surfaces with different orientations, both the opaque but particularly the transparent elements, will significantly influence comfort conditions and energy performance. A relatively simple technique to assess the availability of sunshine on a building façade is to use graphic tools such as the sunpath diagram and shading mask.[7] This allows the designer to plot the path of the sun with respect to topography, vegetation and other obstructions (buildings or shading devices). The intensity of solar radiation in relation to its position in the sky is useful information that allows the designer to judge where to focus the shading or, conversely, the passive solar elements. In cold climates, the aim would be to maximise winter solar gains, while in hot climates it is to minimise gains all year round (Figure 8.3).

8.3 Sunpath diagrams for high (53°N, left) and low (17°N, right) latitude.

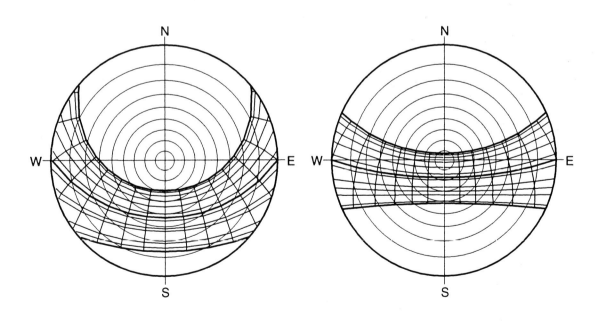

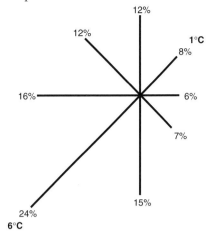

8.4 Example of a simple wind–temperature rose (for January in the South East of England), which reveals not only the prevailing wind directions, but also the associated air temperatures.

Wind

Air movement has an effect both on thermal comfort and energy use. Increasing air movement in warm–humid climates alleviates heat stress, but in hot–arid climates it may increase discomfort by drawing hotter external air into the interior. In moderate climates, air infiltration (unwanted) and ventilation (controlled) can account for a significant fraction of the heating load. In all the above cases, it is important to know the prevailing wind conditions either to maximise the advantages or minimise the disadvantages by manipulating the building design. There are cases where wind may be welcomed from certain directions if it is particularly cool, such as sea breezes in hot–arid regions. In other cases, occupants may need sheltering from cold winds. It is thus necessary to be aware not only of prevailing wind conditions, but also of seasonal wind and the temperature of the wind from different directions (as well as the sand and dust content for arid regions) (Figure 8.4)

Climate data will normally only provide synoptic wind conditions measured at weather stations and at a prescribed height. Such data are useful to provide the overall conditions, but closer site analysis may be necessary. This is particularly true for urban areas where the wind pattern is complex and turbulent.

Pollution

The other microclimatic consideration particularly relevant to the urban context is air and noise pollution. Air pollution is of concern where natural ventilation is the preferred option, although typically the level of some pollutants can be many times greater inside than outside. However, local external pollutant levels may need to be monitored, and may also include levels of dust or sand, to establish either strategic massing and planning responses or detailed ventilation design solutions to achieve natural ventilation in such conditions.

Noise pollution is often quoted as a key issue that challenges the use of natural ventilation in urban areas. The reliance on operable windows for ventilation may cause the admission of unwanted noise. Monitoring such noise levels is necessary to assess the problem and propose solutions through manipulation of the building form, its planning and the design of openings.

Site planning

Spacing

The overall arrangement of buildings on a site should respond to climatic factors such as solar angles and the wind. Where solar access is beneficial to minimise heating loads, then the spacing and orientation of buildings may be informed by solar geometry. Minimising obstruction to the low angle of the winter sun will inform the location of buildings, building heights and separation distances. Sunshine not only is of potential benefit to energy savings in buildings, but also is of importance with respect to the quality of the spaces created between buildings. The typically dense urban fabric of vernacular hot–arid cities reflects the concern of minimising solar radiation in public spaces (Figure 8.5).

With respect to wind, an analysis of speeds, direction and related temperatures will indicate which winds are welcome (e.g. cool summer breezes) and which may be detrimental to comfort and energy efficiency (e.g. cold winter wind). The planning of the site can exploit such conditions by the positioning of buildings and vegetation (as shelter-belts). The dispersed plan of traditional warm–humid towns is a reflection of the need for maximum air movement to maintain comfort. Wind effects, such as channelling and turbulence, caused by buildings will need careful consideration, particularly with tall structures.

8.5 Examples of urban layouts from (left) a high latitude, where solar gains are welcome, and (right) a hot–arid region, where dense urban planning provides mutual shading from the intense sun. *Source (right): Rudofksy 1987.*[8]

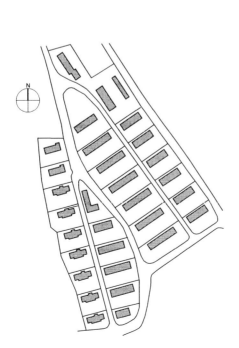

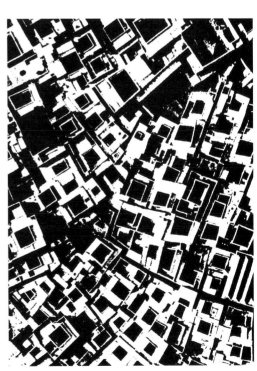

Wind shadows may cause a lack of air movement on the leeward side of buildings. Thus, the interrelationship between buildings needs to be taken into account (Figure 8.6).

8.6 Relationships between the spacing of buildings and wind patterns. *Source:* Goulding *et al.* 1992.[9]

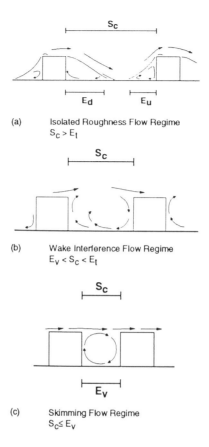

(a)   Isolated Roughness Flow Regime
$S_c > E_t$

(b)   Wake Interference Flow Regime
$E_v < S_c < E_t$

(c)   Skimming Flow Regime
$S_c \leq E_v$

Microclimate

The aim of environmentally responsive planning is not only to *respond* to the climate, but also to *create* a better microclimate as a result of design. Thus, the site plan should contribute to improving the context for the benefit of the overall environment and, in particular, for the benefit of the building itself. For example, the planning of a building site in a noisy, polluted environment may aim to create a quiet protected public space so that parts of the building can be naturally ventilated. This not only reduces the pollution load on the environment, but also creates a haven available for all (Figure 8.7).

8.7 Example of a courtyard plan, where the court is protected from a noisy, polluted environment. *Source: Project Monitor 1987.*[10]

Mixed uses and movement of people

Other, non-climatic issues will have an effect on the resultant energy consumption levels. The location of uses on large sites will influence the need for transport between activities such as housing and offices, or housing and retail, etc. With no mix of uses, it is inevitable that the inhabitants will need to travel (by car or otherwise) outside the development for retail, employment, entertainment, and so on, and will as a result consume energy for such journeys. A dispersed urban plan will typically result in greater use of private vehicular traffic compared with a dense, mixed development.[11]

Another potential advantage of dense mixed-use programmes is that energy supply can be centralised and more efficient. A heating load in one area may be offset by a cooling demand in another. Similarly, a combined heat and power (CHP) plant can supply the mixed demands for hot water and electricity efficiently. The more continuous 24-hour energy demand of mixed-use developments is easy and more efficient to supply locally compared with the intermittent short-term peaks required in single-use zoning (Figure 8.8).

8.8 Masterplan for the Shanghai Central Business District, which proposed a mixed development to reduce peak loads and exploit the greatest potential from combined heat and power (CHP) plants. Architect: Richard Rogers Partnership.

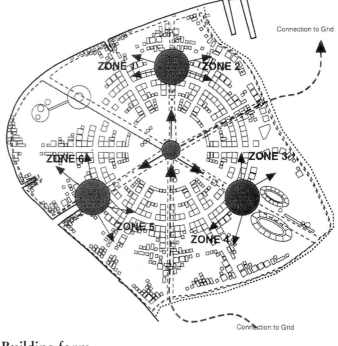

8.9 Example of a building plan (SAS headquarters) with an extensive perimeter and glazed street, which can increase the potential for selective design. Architect: Nils Torp.

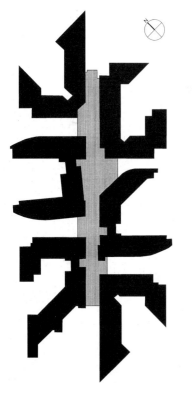

Building form

Passive and non-passive zones

Building form is influential in determining the potential interactions between building environment and climate. To improve energy performance, a building form can be manipulated to exploit those climatic characteristics favourable for human comfort. A building with a high surface-to-volume ratio interacts more with the climate, both potentially positively and negatively. A compact form has less contact with the climate and therefore the internal environment will need to be controlled artificially. In extreme climates, it is often perceived that the less contact with the climate the better, but in terms of energy efficiency a number of opportunities are lost. A simple example of this is the use of controlled natural light to displace the need for artificial lighting energy. Perimeter zones can benefit from access to daylight – as well as natural ventilation and possibly solar gains – and thus contribute to reducing electric lighting loads. Such zones can be called 'potentially passive zones' and the aim in low-energy buildings is to maximise passive zones and minimise non-passive ones.[12]

A building with a high percentage of passive zone will have significantly different form characteristics and will appear elongated, linear, courtyard-like or as a finger plan, as opposed to cuboid. It is clear here that selective environmental design tends to enrich the range of formal possibilities rather than constrain them (Figure 8.9).

Orientation

Building orientation with respect to sunpath and wind direction is relevant whether considering hot climates, where minimising solar gains and maximising air movement may be the priorities, or cold climates, where the reverse effects may be desirable.

In near-equatorial regions where the sunpath is predominantly overhead, radiation on south and north façades can be easily shaded with simple overhangs. However, east and west façades will receive significant direct solar radiation, which is difficult to shade due to the low angles. The most significant aspect is the west elevation as this will receive afternoon sun when air temperatures are at their highest of the day, and this combination of sun and heat will quickly cause overheating problems if not anticipated. A linear building with a west–east axis, where west and east façades are minimised and have minimal openings, is optimum in terms of solar orientation. Wind direction is a secondary issue as façades can be designed and detailed to divert airflow through a building. It is not necessary for the wind direction to be perpendicular, or even near perpendicular, to a façade to encourage airflow to the interior.

In cold regions, solar gains, particularly during the heating season, are welcome. A linear building with a west–east axis is thus also beneficial when solar gains are collected through a solar-oriented façade. Shading from high-altitude summer gains may need to be reduced, particularly in temperate climates, with appropriate shading devices – an overhang for a solar façade being traditional and effective (Figure 8.10).

8.10 Vernacular architecture from a temperate climate region clearly expressing the selective potential of a simple loggia or overhang to provide seasonal solar control. *Source: Rudofsky 1987.*[13]

Internal planning

The internal planning of buildings will have implications on energy and comfort performance. The zoning of, for example, servant areas (e.g. circulation, WCs, plant rooms) as thermal buffer spaces will help to reduce heat losses from the non-solar side and possibly protect the inhabited accommodation from cold winds. Conversely, thermal buffer spaces can be used to protect an interior from excessive solar gains so that, for example, the west or east façades of buildings can be protected from low-angle afternoon or morning sun (Figure 8.11).

8.11 The plan of this office building (IBM Plaza, Kuala Lumpur, Malaysia) has service spaces on the west façade to protect the accommodation from the afternoon summer sun. Architect: Ken Yeang. *Source:* Hamzah and Yeang 1994.[14]

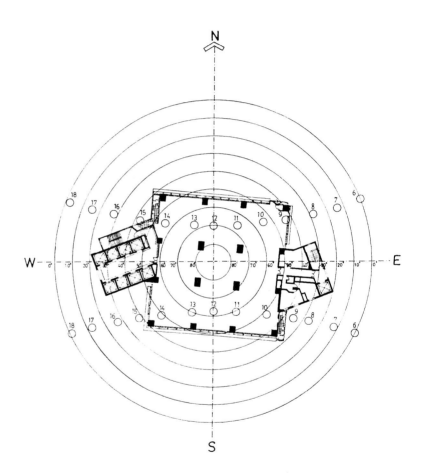

Noise-generating areas of the accommodation (e.g. plant rooms, machine rooms, workshops) act as acoustic buffer spaces and can protect the rest of the building from a noisy context as well as allowing it to be potentially naturally ventilated.

Courts and atria

Before the advent of air-conditioning and deep-plan buildings, courtyards and light wells were used widely to provide both ventilation and natural light to otherwise deep-plan urban buildings. The benefits in terms of energy use of reducing the need for fan power and artificial light are self-evident. Further advantages may include improved occupant well-being and productivity,[15] and reduced costs by the avoidance of air-conditioning systems. Typological studies of built form and site densities have also indicated that courts can improve the plot ratios of developments.[16]

The renewed interest in courts, and particularly in glazed courts or atria, provides opportunities for low-energy strategies, which are briefly outlined below.

Thermal buffer

The first advantage of a glazed atrium over an open court is that heat losses from the building are reduced. This is because the extent of the external envelope directly in contact with the outside is reduced. Heat losses from the building and solar gains into the atrium will ensure that the atrium temperature is likely to be always higher than outside temperature. This means that fabric losses from the building into the atrium are reduced. This is known as the thermal buffer effect of atria.

Daylight

By puncturing an atrium through the plan of a deep building, natural light can reach more of the accommodation. The reflectances of the surfaces are under the control of the designer, unlike adjacent street façades, and can therefore be light-coloured to maximise daylight penetration. In the case where a court is glazed over, the structure of the glazing system and the glass itself will reduce the amount of light transmitted. However, in such a case the atrium temperatures are higher than the outside and therefore heat loss from the building will be reduced. This in turn means that glazing ratios can afford to be larger to improve daylight without a heat loss penalty.

Ventilation

The advantage of court plans is that the cross-section from façade to façade can be reduced down to a distance where cross-ventilation becomes possible. Typically, this distance is taken to be in the order of 12 metres. Cross-ventilation requires there to be a pressure difference between the façades, normally provided by wind. However, in still wind conditions, air movement in buildings is governed by thermal buoyancy. Where a court is glazed over, the wind effects are likely to be reduced, but the potential for a stack-effect (thermal buoyancy) is increased where stack heights become significant (i.e. an atrium of at least six stories). The height of the atrium assists the stack-driven ventilation, assuming that openings are provided at the top of the atrium for warm air to escape. This effect induces fresh air to be introduced from the perimeter of the building, across the accommodation and into the atrium. The necessary summer ventilation rate can thus be maintained even under the worst-case conditions of no wind. Opening location and sizes need to be carefully designed to ensure adequate and controllable ventilation rates.

Where the main energy use in a building is for space heating, then an alternative ventilation strategy can be adopted to minimise winter heating loads. The warm air in the atrium can be usefully used as preheated ventilation air for adjacent accommodation. The atrium is kept sealed to the outside and the warmed air is encouraged to enter the building. In this way, thermal losses through ventilation, which in a well-insulated design account for the largest fraction of heat loss, can be reduced. Any solar gains made into the atrium space during the winter become very useful. It is important when adopting such a strategy to consider the ventilation paths carefully, both in terms of location and sizing.

Building use

Occupancy patterns and behaviour

The way buildings are used by occupants has a profound impact on energy use. It is not simply a direct relationship between hours of occupancy and resultant energy use, but relates to the behavioural patterns of occupants and the thermal mass characteristics of the building fabric. Occupants can change the energy performance of identical buildings by a factor of 2 as a result of opening windows, misuse of heating or air-conditioning controls, and switching on/off of artificial lighting. Buildings with a continuous occupancy pattern (i.e. 24-hour use) may benefit from a high-level thermal mass, dependent on climatic variations. Short-term, intermittent occupancy will demand rapid control of the environmental conditions, which suggests a lightweight structure and a fast response system.

In the design of passive control systems (operable windows, movable shading, light switching, etc.), consideration of occupant behaviour must be taken into account. A robust strategy where building performance is supported by likely occupant response is an important notion. Simple, effective and direct manual control will provide the user with confidence and increased satisfaction. If control of the environment is obscured, the occupant is likely to feel less comfortable and also more likely to interact inappropriately. In such a case, fully automated control will provide better performance. Consider ventilation as an example. In the case where ventilation is provided through operable windows, occupants will tend to open windows to increase ventilation as necessary (although they may not turn the heating off, or leave the window open longer than necessary). If, however, fresh air is delivered through a grille in the ceiling and controlled via a thermostat, then users may resort to turning controls excessively, opening doors or switching on fans to increase air movement. The results may be noise and privacy problems and a perceived reduced comfort level. An integrated system where temperature sensors open and close windows automatically, but can be overridden manually, may prove the most effective solution.

Environmental requirements

The environmental requirements of various uses need to be established and can have a significant influence on design strategy. This is particularly important in mixed-use buildings. A simple example of this may be an office building with computer rooms, administrative offices, drawing studios and social spaces. Each area, therefore, has differing requirements in terms of light. Computer rooms do not need high levels of natural light but require careful glare consideration. Drawing studios benefit from higher levels of daylight, while social spaces may benefit from sunlight. The plan organisation of such spaces will thus relate to their environmental requirements: computer suites on the ground floor, drawing office top lit, administration in between, and social spaces on the sunny side.

Similarly, thermal criteria and noise issues will inform appropriate planning decisions, and the use of buffer spaces to protect the more environmentally sensitive areas. The notion of selective design thus not only has a baring on early design decisions of built form, but also transcends through all the design stages and levels of detail.

Different spaces and activities will require different levels of environmental control, ranging from aiming to maintain temperatures at 20 ± 1°C for sensitive equipment and materials to allowing temperatures to swing between 18 and 27°C for human comfort. Similarly, humidity levels and the need for cleaning and filtering air will vary according to building use. Such considerations will influence decisions about the level of mechanical services and their specifications.

Internal gains and light levels

The levels of internal gains relate directly to building use and are a function of equipment, occupancy and lighting systems. For example, in an office where computer use is intense, internal gains will be significant. Similarly, in spaces designed for dense occupancy, such as classrooms, lecture rooms and auditoria, internal gains are high for certain periods, and such spaces will require high levels of ventilation air for health and comfort. In spaces where high light levels are required, heat gains will need to be assessed. Clearly, internal gains will depend on the efficiency of the lighting system and whether daylight can be used to minimise the load.

Building fabric

Insulation and U values

Thermal insulation is a primary way of avoiding heat loss from buildings. It is thus essential to consider levels of insulation where the heating load is a major fraction of the energy bill. In cases where internal gains are high, it is likely that the heating load is not significant. Therefore, the emphasis of an energy-efficient strategy will be on avoiding the need for cooling rather than on minimising heat loss. Similarly, in hot climates, this will also be the case, although thermal insulation can play an important role in reducing solar gains through the fabric.

For example, current UK Building Regulations stipulate maximum U values and maximum glazing ratios to minimise fabric heat losses. This may be appropriate for domestic buildings, but the conditions in non-domestic buildings require a more sophisticated response to energy efficiency, including the consideration of daylighting, shading and natural ventilation. These issues will clearly affect the nature and composition of the building fabric.

Thermal mass and surface resistance

The amount and distribution of thermal mass in the building fabric will affect the thermal response and performance of the spaces. A heavyweight building will respond slowly to heat gains, either from the heating system or from other sources such as solar and internal gains. This can be advantageous at both delaying and reducing the peak temperatures caused by such heat gains. However, some building types with short occupancy patterns will benefit from a lightweight fabric. If well insulated, such a building will have a fast response and thus will not require a long lead-in time to warm up.

Thermal mass can also be of use to increase the temperature usefully during occupancy. For example, in housing in cold climates, solar gains can be absorbed into the mass during the day and released in the evening. Thus, comfort conditions can be maintained for a longer part of the day before resorting to artificial heating sources.

In terms of energy use, thermal mass only has potential benefits if the services are designed for it. For example, a fully air-conditioned building will not benefit significantly in energy terms from thermal mass as most of the energy is required for fan power. However, in mixed-mode buildings, where passive design is integrated with systems, cooling can be avoided until peak temperatures rise. Thermal mass will delay the need for cooling, thus shortening the cooling season.

Where thermal mass is used, thickness and surface area are significant characteristics. The thicker the mass, the longer the time lag. If a large surface area is available, then mass will be more effective.

Embodied energy and toxicity of materials

New environmental issues raised with respect to the choice of building materials relate to energy use in their manufacture and transport, and to the health issues of materials and their treatment (paints, varnishes, etc.) after construction.

The materials used in construction have gone through various processes before being integrated on site. Such processes consume various amounts of energy, which are 'embodied' in the final building material. High-process elements, such as aluminium, steel and glass, have more embodied energy per cubic metre than, for example, concrete or timber. Another aspect that may contribute to the choice of materials or elements in buildings is the transport energy required to deliver the product. Clearly, locally made products will require less transport energy than those imported from abroad. The embodied energy in a building in Europe or North America is typically equivalent to five times the amount of annual energy required to operate the building.

The choice of materials may also relate to health considerations, both in terms of the fabrication processes of products and when installed in buildings. For example, the 'off-gassing' of volatile organic compounds into a space can increase internal pollution levels to ten times outside levels. The lower ventilation rates caused by modern construction techniques and adopted to minimise energy loss exacerbate the problem. Dust collected in carpets and soft furnishings will increase the population of dust mites, whose faeces can cause irritation, allergic reactions and generally reduce the well-being of occupants.

Daylighting

Natural light and the daylight factor

Lighting goes to the heart of the architectural enterprise. Electric lighting can also account for the largest single primary energy load in buildings, thus any reduced reliance on artificial light can make significant energy savings. This can be achieved by displacing the need for artificial light by daylight. Daylight factors of ≥ 2% can reduce energy use for lighting by about 60% compared with a totally artificially lit space. However, to achieve daylight levels throughout a building requires careful planning. Clearly, deep-plan designs will not achieve daylighting deep into the plan. Typically, a perimeter depth of 6 metres, or twice the floor-to-ceiling height, can be potentially daylit. Thus, buildings deeper than 12 metres may require more artificial light. However, the darker central areas are often assigned as circulation space, requiring only low levels of light. Other darker plan areas can be occupied by secondary spaces such as services, WCs and storage areas.

Innovative devices such as light shelves, light ducts, reflectors, holographic films, fibreoptics, etc., can be adopted to increase the penetration of natural light.

For daylight strategies to be effective in terms of energy savings, it is essential that automatic switching is adopted to ensure that artificial lights are off when sufficient daylight is available.

Light distribution

The degree of penetration is not only in terms of achieving good levels of light deep in the plan, but also that light distribution is significant in determining visual comfort and how occupants are likely to switch lights. An even distribution and high level of light will tend to make the whole space well lit. However, this is often difficult to achieve as light levels tend to drop off quickly further away from windows. If the back part of a room appears significantly darker (e.g. by a factor of 5) than the front part of a room, then it will appear gloomy even if light levels are high. It is thus the relative brightness that is important. In conditions of poor light distribution, occupants are likely to turn lights on at the back of the room. Light distribution can be improved by devices such as light shelves, which, although they do not increase light levels at the back, do reduce levels near the window, resulting in a more even distribution. Shading devices often tend to worsen the light distribution unless carefully designed (e.g. louvered and light-coloured).

Glazing distribution

It is not only the amount of glazing that determines daylighting conditions in a space. The positioning of windows will influence light distribution. High-level windows will give a better daylight penetration compared with low-level windows. Similarly, tall windows will throw light deeper into the plan than wide windows of the same area. As a simple rule of thumb, this effect can be demonstrated by determining the no-sky line. If from any point the sky cannot be seen, it is likely that daylight levels will drop quickly. The no-sky line is thus a good indication of the depth of daylight penetration.

Views, glare, privacy and thermal balance

Window design clearly has to perform a number of tasks including those mentioned above. A resolution of all the issues is complex and therefore priorities have to be taken to arrive at a satisfactory compromise. In terms of energy use, buildings occupied during the day and requiring good lighting will be dominated by the need for daylight. However, in, for example, housing, thermal issues (solar gains versus heat loss) as well as views will be more important.

Passive solar gains

Useful solar gains

Where buildings have heating requirements, the thermal load can be reduced by designing for solar gains. The design of passive solar architecture requires an understanding of solar geometry and seasonal heat loads. For example, it is most likely that peak loads coincide with low sun angles. Thus, solar-oriented, vertically glazed openings may be particularly effective at collecting gains in the winter, whilst horizontal openings will collect more gains when solar altitudes are high (i.e. in the summer) and air temperatures are high. Passive solar buildings are typically characterised by large solar-oriented windows and small openings to the non-solar façade.

On a daily cycle, it becomes important to consider the sun's position in relation to external temperatures. A morning, easterly sun may be very useful as ambient air temperatures are low. However, an evening westerly sun should be controlled as it will otherwise contribute to internal gains when outside temperatures are at their highest. The direct solar gain strategies mentioned above require careful control. The issue of solar control is discussed below.

Glazed spaces in the form of conservatories or atria can be used to collect gains indirectly before those gains are transferred into the building or ventilated directly out if unwanted. Thus, indirect solar strategies offer greater control.

The planning of buildings to respond to orientation is necessary. The main habitable areas should be oriented to the solar side, with perhaps the kitchen oriented to receive the morning sun and the living space facing the afternoon and early evening sun. Secondary spaces such as circulation space, bathrooms and garages can be situated on the non-solar side, requiring only small windows and lower temperatures. Such spaces would thus act as a thermal buffer.

Distribution

Once solar gains have been collected in the building, either by direct or indirect gains, it is important to distribute them efficiently to other spaces to get the greatest benefit (or solar utilisation) from those gains. In a direct gain design, the distribution of gains from the solar to the non-solar side can be assisted by ventilation strategies. For example, the design of a stairwell as a thermal flue on the non-solar side will draw warm air across the plan from the solar side. Similarly, where mechanical extract is required in kitchens and bathrooms, the negative pressure can be used to encourage air movement in certain directions.

Where solar gains are made indirectly into a sunspace, then it is important to link this space to as many of the other spaces in the house via ventilation openings. Double-height conservatories are often used to enable this direct link to other floors. Thus, the ventilation air for the spaces is preheated in the sunspace by solar gains and drawn directly from the sunspace to other areas.

Control and comfort

Solar control is essential where large areas of glazing are adopted. In terms of fixed devices, on solar façades a simple overhang will intercept the high-angle summer sun, but on east and west façades the sun's angle is lower and control becomes more important. A more elaborate device such as egg crates is appropriate, or in lower latitudes the avoidance of glazing on such orientations may be necessary to minimise overheating risks. On non-solar façades, shading is often minimal in the form of vertical fins to intercept oblique sunlight in summer. Often it will be unnecessary to shade non-solar façades depending on the level of internal gains and summer peak temperatures.

It is recommended that moveable devices be used to allow for greater control. The climate is not totally predictable and great fluctuations in temperature and solar radiation are likely. To ensure that comfort conditions are maintained, louvered systems or retractable blinds are recommended. A degree of occupant control over their own environmental conditions will help to improve their perception of comfort, and their acceptance of a wider comfort range.

Natural ventilation

Wind and stack-effect

There are basically three levels of requirement with respect to natural ventilation: to provide fresh air (health); to provide air movement for convective and evaporative cooling from the human body (comfort); and to dissipate heat from a building without the need for air-conditioning (energy efficiency). The first demands only low levels of air infiltration; the second requires noticeable air movement carefully designed to pass across the occupied space; while the third suggests the need for high ventilation rates at high level to remove accumulated heat and cool the thermal mass of a building.

The two available mechanisms for providing air movement are the wind and stack-induced effects. The wind is often unpredictable, although designs should consider prevailing directions and opening positions. Wind pressures are likely to be larger than stack pressures and thus can contribute to providing high ventilation rates. However, during periods of low wind, the stack-effect may provide the only source of air movement through the effect of thermal buoyancy. Warm air rises and, if stacks are designed correctly, the effect can be exploited to generate sufficient air movement for comfort cooling. The stack-effect is determined by the stack height between the top and lower openings (the higher, the greater the pressure difference), by opening size (the larger, the greater the air flow), and the temperature difference between inside and outside (the larger, the greater the pressure difference).

Night-time cooling

To maximise the benefit of thermal mass, night-time cooling will 'purge' heat from the structure, cooling it down in preparation for the next day's occupation. For night-time cooling to be effective, the ventilation air must have maximum contact with the thermal mass. Any obstructions, for example to an exposed mass ceiling by down stands or light fittings, will redirect the air flow away from the mass, thus reducing its effectiveness. The location of openings with respect to thermal mass is relevant for the same reason. The stack-effect can often be relied upon to evacuate heat if night-time temperatures are lower than average internal temperatures, and in other situations the wind may be the main driving force for ventilation. Finally, openings should be protected for security reasons.

Noise and atmospheric pollution

The aim of ventilation to provide fresh air for health and comfort can be jeopardised if the source of air is polluted or noisy. Pollution and noise are often quoted as the reasons for using air-conditioning, particularly in urban environments. However, although noise and air pollution impose constraints on possible design solutions, there are techniques to minimise the problems.

With respect to noise, the way air enters a building can be manipulated to minimise noise transference (e.g. increasing the path length, using both acoustically lined ducts and acoustic shelves outside windows, and the positioning of acoustic-absorbent panels on surfaces inside). It may be that certain areas of a site require particularly careful acoustic consideration, but the site can be protected by the design of the building form, allowing other areas to be naturally ventilated. Those areas on the noisy edge may be the ones that require mechanical ventilation in any case, and thus serve as a buffer for the rest of the building.

The problem of air pollution can be tackled by building form in a similar way as that described above. The creation of protected courtyards and planting to help settle out and filter dust particles may be considered. The source of incoming air should be removed from the polluted areas, perhaps raised to the top of the building where any pollution is more diluted.

Overheating and comfort

Window sizing

To minimise the risk of overheating from solar gains, the area and orientation of glazing needs to respond to the amount and timing of radiation. In temperate climates, the aim is to control summer gains, particularly in buildings with high internal casual gains. Overheating in such a case is most likely to occur in the early afternoon when external temperatures are highest. If a

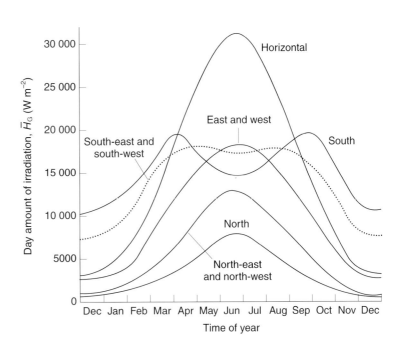

8.12 Example, at latitude 52°N, of the amount of solar radiation falling on building façades of different orientations, indicating that horizontal, west and east façades receive peak summer time radiation. *Source:* Marks and Morris 1980.[17]

building has west-facing windows, then low-angle afternoon solar gains will enter the building and add to internal gains. East-facing glazing is not such a problem as generally air temperatures are lower and solar gains may usefully contribute to warming the building in the morning. On solar-oriented windows, only a fraction of the solar radiation available will be transmitted to the interior because of the high solar altitude and oblique angle of incidence. The amount of solar radiation on such façades peaks during the spring and autumn months (Figure 8.12).

In hot climates nearer the Equator, west- and east-facing windows should be avoided.

Shading devices

Shading devices are an essential technique of avoiding unwanted solar gains, but they need to respond in design to orientation (see 'Control and comfort' above). Fixed devices are rarely sufficient to control sunshine and are often required not only for thermal control, but also for glare control.

Ventilation strategies

To provide comfort, solar shading must be integrated with a ventilation strategy. The design of the window to perform the functions of solar shading, glare control, provision of natural light and source of ventilation air needs careful consideration. Shading systems must not interfere with ventilation flow or increase air temperatures locally. An example of this is may be a 'brise soleil', which, although it intercepts unwanted solar radiation, ironically heats up incoming air as it flows over the solar-warmed device.

The provision of high- and low-level openings will ensure that the stack-effect will induce ventilation when there is no wind. Further, in a situation where cross-ventilation is achieved, then high- and low-level openings provide control of ventilation for the three levels discussed above, that is health, comfort and energy efficiency. A single opening ensures top-up fresh air for health, low-level openings help provide air movement across the occupied zone and high-level windows are appropriately located for high rates of ventilation (above the occupied zone) for dissipation of heat and for night-time cooling. Ventilation strategies are described in more detail in 'Natural ventilation' above.

Thermal mass

Thermal mass, as discussed above in 'Building fabric', assists in reducing peak temperatures and therefore is useful in reducing the likely risk of overheating. Apart from reducing air temperature, another mechanism at work which is more important with respect to comfort is that mean radiant temperature (MRT) is potentially reduced. Comfort is dependent on MRT and the lower surface temperature of thermal mass will reduce MRT and make higher air temperature more tolerable. However, for the effect of thermal mass to be noticeable, it must be exposed.

Artificial lighting

Controls: manual or automated

The use of natural light to displace the need for artificial light can have significant potential energy benefits (see 'Daylighting'), but it is dependent on lamps being switched off when not required. Manual switching cannot be relied upon, particularly in open-plan buildings, but there are alternative switching controls ranging in complexity, including:

- time switching off/manual on;
- photoelectric switching off/manual on;
- photoelectric switching on/off;
- photoelectric dimming; and
- occupancy sensors (movement or noise).

Each has significant energy-saving potential and is appropriate in different circumstances. Economic appraisals have shown that automatic switching can be cost-effective in both new and existing buildings.

Lamps and luminaires

A simple strategy for reducing lighting loads is to adopt low-energy lamps with higher efficacies. This generally results in the use of fluorescent lamps, both in tubular form or as compact lamps suitable for a wider range of fittings. The choice of fittings will also play a role in how effectively the light is distributed and, therefore, have implications on energy use.

Efficacy and internal gains

The choice of efficient lamps and luminaires means that more light can be obtained for less heat output. The amount of fittings can thus be reduced, which in turn reduces the level of internal gains. If daylight is relied upon for a substantial time of the occupied period, internal gains from lights will be minimal. A consequence will be a reduced cooling load or even the avoidance of air-conditioning.

Heating

Fuel and plant

Fuel choice is often limited to what is available but should be considered in terms of environmental impact. Thus, in the UK, the use of gas for heating is typically three times more energy efficient (both in terms of cost and pollutants) than electricity. However, where electricity is generated by, for example, hydropower, the balance of this simple comparison changes greatly. The use of renewable sources of energy such as solar and wind power should be assessed early on in the design to allow full architectural integration.

Once the source of energy has been determined, the nature of the heating plant will play an important role in terms of energy efficiency. Although this guide will not provide detailed comparisons of plant, the location, zoning and distribution of heat is important. The planning of a heating plant should reflect the use and occupancy patterns of a building. The first step is to zone the heating system according to use. This will involve considering whether the plant should be centralised or decentralised. Furthermore, boilers should not be operating at low efficiencies when only a small part of the building is occupied but should be sized to run at near full capacity. If the load reduces, then banks of boilers can be turned off so that even when loads are small, heat can be provided efficiently.

Emitters

The choice of heat emitters is important both in terms of their efficiency (minimal energy for maximum comfort) and integration with the building fabric. Comfort is determined by a combination of radiant and convective conditions. Any strong asymmetry in these conditions will reduce comfort. Thus, if heat emitters rely solely on transferring heat by convection, an improvement of the radiant environment should be considered (e.g. use of an emitter with a radiant heat output component, use of thermal mass or solar energy). Most heat emitters combine heat output via convection and radiation. For example, a 'radiator' will radiate 40% of heat but will cause convection currents across it which transfer 60% of the heat to the room air.

Distribution

The distribution of thermal energy is again an issue that will affect energy efficiency and design integration. It may be that a totally decentralised plant is appropriate, where heat is generated and provided at the location where needed. However, where systems are centralised, efficient control and maintenance become more effective. Heat reclamation may also require a more centralised plant for maximum efficiency so that excess heat from one area can be reclaimed for an area with high loads.

Location

In the same way that spaces are planned and linked by circulation routes, so a heating system and its emitters will need to be planned. However, the planning of the system and location of plant, distribution runs and emitters needs to be integrated and sympathetic to the overall architectural and environmental aims of the design. There are some simple rules such as that heat emitters should be positioned under windows to minimise discomfort from downdrafts and counterbalance radiative losses through glazing.

Services

Need for air-conditioning

The avoidance of air-conditioning can make very significant energy savings, thus there is a need to address the question of whether air-conditioning is needed. Can comfort be achieved by passive means? Often, air-conditioning is seen to be necessary for reasons such as guaranteeing temperature conditions between 19 and 21°C. It is known that comfort conditions range from about 19 to 27°C, so that if such criteria are used, cooling may be unnecessary for all or large parts of the building. The use of shading devices, thermal mass, shallow plans for daylight and natural ventilation, planning for noise, etc., are all techniques that reduce and potentially eliminate the need for air-conditioning.

Mechanical ventilation

It may be possible to avoid air-conditioning by largely passive means and to use mechanical ventilation (i.e. no cooling) only to provide fresh air for heat dissipation and evaporative cooling.

Mixed-mode and zoning

Although there may be spaces in the design where internal loads or other considerations demand the need for air-conditioning, it is unnecessary to air-condition the whole building. Certain areas may be ideal for natural ventilation, while others will only require some mechanical ventilation. Thus, the zoning of such areas and the notion of mixed-mode systems design can save significant amounts of energy use.

Integration

The integration of services, whether hidden or expressed, is important for successful design. The choice of the air-conditioning system will affect the complexity of integration. For example, an all-air system requires larger volumes for the integration of ductwork compared with a refrigerant system with its chilled water pipes and local air handling. Similarly, a centralised plant will require larger and longer pipe and duct runs, which will need to be carefully planned in conjunction with the structure and fabric of the building. As Louis Kahn said:

I do not like ducts, I do not like pipes. I hate them really thoroughly, I feel that they have to be given their place. If I just hated them and took no care, I think that they would invade the building and completely destroy it.[18]

References

1 Steen E. Rasmussen, *Experiencing Architecture*, MIT Press, Cambridge, MA, 1984.

2 World Commission on Environment and Development, *Our Common Future.* 'Bruntland Report'. Oxford University Press, Oxford, 1987.

3 W. T. Bordass, A. K. R. Bromley and A. J. Leaman, *Comfort, Control and Energy Efficiency in Offices.* BRE IP3/95, February 1995.

4 A. Rapoport, *House Form and Culture*, Prentice Hall, Englewood Cliffs, NJ, 1969.

5 H. E. Landsberg, *The Urban Climate*, Academic Press, London, 1981.

6 P. Achard and R. Gicquel (eds.), *European Passive Solar Handbook: Basic Principles and Concepts for Passive Solar Architecture*, Preliminary edition, CEC, p. 2.19, EUR 10 683, 1986.

7 J. R. Goulding, J. O. Lewis and T. C. Steemers, *Energy in Architecture: The European Passive Solar Handbook*, B. T. Batsford, London, 1992.

8 B. Rudofsky, *Architecture Without Architects: A Short Introduction to Non-Pedigreed Architecture*, University of New Mexico Press, Albuquerque, fig. no. 54 (reprint), 1987. Originally published, Museum of Modern Art, New York, 1964.

9 J. R. Goulding, J. O. Lewis and T. C. Steemers (eds.), *Energy in Architecture: A European Passive Solar Handbook*, Batsford, London, 1992, p. 33.

10 'Braircliff House, Farnborough, UK', *Project Monitor*, CEC, Issue 12, December, 1987, p. 4.

11 H. Sherlock, *Cities Are Good For Us*, Paladin, London, 1991.

12 N. V. Baker and K. Steemers, *Energy and Environment in Architecture*, E & FN Spon/Routledge, London, 2000.

13 B. Rudofsky, *Architecture Without Architects: A Short Introduction to Non-Pedigreed Architecture*, University of New Mexico Press, Albuquerque, fig. no. 88 (reprint), 1987. Originally published, Museum of Modern Art, New York, 1964.

14 T. R. Hamzah and K. Yeang, *Bioclimatic Skyscrapers*, 2nd edition, Ellipsis, London, 1994 (1st edition published 1994).

15 D. Clements-Croome (ed.), *Creating the Productive Workplace*, E&FN Spon, 2000.

16 L. Martin and L. March (eds), *Urban Space and Structures*, Cambridge University Press, Cambridge, 1972.

17 T. A. Marks and E. N. Morris, *Buildings, Climate and Energy*, Pitman Publishing., London, 1980, p. 200.

18 Louis I. Kahn, quoted in R. Banham, *The Architecture of a Well-Tempered Environment*, Architectural Press, London, 1969, p. 249.

Select bibliography

This bibliography presents a critical review of literature that has informed the production of this book. The majority of the sources are explicitly referred to in the main text, but others, while not given formal citation, are, in the authors' view, essential texts in establishing the wider context within which we have undertaken our project.

C. Abel, *Architecture and Identity*, Architectural Press/Butterworth-Heinemann, Oxford, 1997. This collection of essays includes some important studies on the question of the relationship between modern science and architecture and, of particular relevance in the present context, the cultural conflicts of globalisation.

P. Achard and R. Gicquel (eds), *European Passive Solar Handbook*, Commission of the European Communities, 1986. One of the most comprehensive references for the fundamentals of passive solar principles applied to the context of Northern Europe. The emphasis is upon the use of solar energy for space heating.

D. Anink, C. Boonstra and J. Mack, *Handbook of Sustainable Building: An Environmental Preference Method for Selection of Materials for Use in Construction and Refurbishment*, James & James, London, 1996.

Nick V. Baker and K. Steemers, *The LT Method v 2.0*, Cambridge Architectural Research and The Martin Centre for Architectural and Urban Studies, Cambridge, 1994. A manual design tool for the calculation of energy demand in non-domestic buildings in the European context. The method integrates the consumption of energy for heating, cooling and illumination in a clear and comprehensible way.

Rayner Banham, *The Architecture of the Well-Tempered Environment*, Architectural Press, London, 1969. The first significant attempt at a history of the development of environmental systems in architecture. The book laid the foundations for the emergence of an environmentally oriented extension of the history of architecture in the nineteenth and twentieth centuries.

R. G. Barry and R. J. Chorley, *Atmosphere, Weather and Climate*, Routledge, London, 1968, 6th edn 1992. A thorough introduction to weather processes and climatic conditions in all the climate regions of the globe.

T. Binns, *Tropical Africa*, Routledge, London. Case studies on the relation of population and environment in rural and urban Africa.

B. E. Bourges (ed.), *Climatic Data Handbook for Europe*, Kluwer, Dordrecht, 1992. Presents a comprehensive set of data on solar radiation, temperatures, degree-days and other parameters for a great number of European locations.

Ken Butti and John Perlin, *A Golden Thread: 2500 Years of Solar Architecture*, Cheshire, Palo Alto, CA, 1980. A pioneering account of the relationship between architecture and climate throughout history.

Derek Clements-Croome (ed.), *Naturally Ventilated Buildings: Buildings for the Senses, the Economy and Society*. E & FN Spon, London, 1997. A collection of essays by British authors that approaches the problem of the naturally ventilated building from diverse points of view: technical, behavioural and aesthetic.

Alan Colquhoun, *Essays in Architectural Criticism: Modern Architecture and Historical Change*. MIT Press, Cambridge, MA, 1981. An important collection of critical essays that encapsulates the emergence of a critical perspective on the architecture of the Modern Movement. Includes seminal studies on the role of typology in architecture and on the relationship between technology and representation.

G. Conklin, *The Weather Conditioned House*, Reinhold, New York, 1958. An early attempt to present architectural science in simple, comprehensive language. The goal of presenting the air-conditioned house as 'living companionably with the natural environment' is now clearly anachronistic.

R. W. Crump and M. Harms (eds), *The Design Connection: Energy and Technology in Architecture*, van Nostrand Reinhold, New York, 1981. Lectures delivered at Cornell University in 1978 by distinguished theoreticians and practitioners, including James Marston Fitch, Ralph Erskine and Ralph Knowles.

Susan Denyer, *African Traditional Architecture: An Historical and Geographical Perspective*, Heinemann, London, 1978. A survey of traditional architecture of Africa and an investigation into its genesis and subsequent twentieth-century interpretation. It has well-catalogued photographs and analytical sketches showing dwelling types, constructional methods.

J. Farmer (ed. K. Richardson), *Green Shift: Towards a Green Sensibility in Architecture*, Butterworth Architecture, London, 1996. A wide-ranging exploration of the historical relationship between architecture and nature from the eighteenth century to the end of the twentieth. The particular value of the book lies in its location of contemporary environmental concerns, both local and global, in the context of cultural history and, thereby, offering an alternative perspective from that provided by architectural science.

H. Fathy, *Natural Energy and Vernacular Architecture: Principles and Examples with Reference to Hot Arid Climates*, University of Chicago Press, Chicago, IL, 1986. A key work by a major practitioner and theoretician. It presents an elegant outline of fundamental principles and summarises all the climatic factors that bear upon architectural design in hot–arid climates, and discusses the nature of comfort and traditional mechanisms for humidification. The emphasis is upon the design of housing and illustrations are predominantly drawn from vernacular architecture. Contains a detailed description of mashrabiya.

James Marston Fitch, *American Building: 2: The Environmental Forces That Shape It*, Houghton Mifflin, Boston, MA, 1972. One of the classic texts exploring the question of environmental regionalism in architecture. Analysis of the American vernacular is developed to provide the basis for an analytical procedure for the production of designs, which are adapted to the climatic context.

Kenneth Frampton (ed. John Cava), *Studies in Tectonic Culture: The Poetics of Construction in Nineteenth and Twentieth Century Architecture*, MIT Press, Cambridge, MA, 1995. An important study of the relationship between technology and the creative processes of architecture. It is particularly important in its assertion that the relationship between tectonics, and by implication all technologies, and architectural form and style is not deterministic.

B. Givoni, *Man, Climate and Architecture*, Applied Science, London, 1969, 2nd edn 1976. One of the seminal works of architectural science. The emphasis is upon the fundamentals of the physical processes that determine the climate response of buildings. Detailed exposition of mathematical relationships and empirical investigations. Abstract and rigorous.

B. Givoni, *Passive and Low Energy Cooling of Buildings*, van Nostrand Reinhold, New York, 1994. Givoni brings his rigorous scientific approach to this key account of the fundamentals of cooling buildings without the use of air-conditioning. In the context of 'selective' design in hot climates, it is essential to maximise the potential of the building fabric and of passive processes.

G. S. Golany, *Design for Arid Regions*, van Nostrand Reinhold, New York, 1983. A collection of papers concerned primarily with the requirements for urban design in arid regions. Contains a comprehensive set of illustrations of vernacular methods of climate control.

J. R. Goulding, J. O. Lewis and T. C. Steemer (eds) *Energy in Architecture: A European Passive Solar Handbook*, revd, B. T. Batsford, London, 1992. The revised version of this important document, which remains a primary source in the field.

Dean Hawkes and Janet Owers (eds), *The Architecture of Energy*, Construction Press/Longman, Harlow, 1982. The proceedings of an international conference held in Cambridge in 1980, the papers cover aspects of theoretical development and innovative practice of the period. The emphasis is upon the design of non-domestic building types, office buildings, schools and industrial buildings.

Dean Hawkes, *The Environmental Tradition: Studies in the Architecture of Environment*, E & FN Spon, London, 1996. A collection of essays on both the theory and practice of environmental design. The overriding concern is to locate the contemporary environmental debate in the wider field of the history and theory of architecture. The architectural references include the works of Arup Associates, Sir Charles Barry, Louis Kahn, Charles Rennie Mackintosh, Sir Leslie Martin and Robert Venturi.

Thomas Herzog (ed.), *Solar Energy in Architecture and Planning*, Prestel, Berlin, 1996. Produced to accompany the technical *Proceedings of the European Conference on Architecture*, the conference of which was held in Berlin in 1996, this beautifully produced and illustrated book brings together a selection of projects by internationally acknowledged architects, including Norman Foster, Jourda and Perraudin, Renzo Piano, Richard Rogers and Thomas Herzog himself. These designs show how environmentally responsive principles may be incorporated in the design of buildings for many functions.

R. G. Hopkinson, *Architectural Physics: Lighting*, HMSO, London, 1963. Hopkinson was one of the great architectural scientists and this book remains one of the best texts on the fundamentals of daylighting in buildings.

Ralph Knowles, *Energy and Form: An Ecological Approach to Urban Growth*, MIT Press, Cambridge, MA, 1974. One of the major works of the modern environmental movement in architecture. Knowles's work makes explicit the relationship between access to solar energy and the development of the built form.

Ralph Knowles, *Sun, Rhythm, Form*, MIT Press, Cambridge, MA, 1981. A poetic exploration of the significance of the sun's seasonal and diurnal rhythms for architectural form.

O. H. Koenigsberger *et al.*, *Manual of Tropical Housing and Building: Part One – Climatic Design*, Longman, London, 1974. One of the standard references deriving from the colonial tradition. Contains a great amount of objective and relevant data for design in the tropics.

U. Kulturman, *New Architecture in Africa*, Thames & Hudson, London, 1963. An essentially pictorial and descriptive review of late modernist buildings in Africa designed by both African and European architects. Argues for the need to discover an architectural expression of the new sense of African identity that followed the moves towards political independence of the period.

H. E. Landsberg (editor-in-chief), *World Survey of Climatology*, Elsevier, Amsterdam. This series constitutes one of the major works of reference that stands as context to the issues of global architectural design. The data are clearly and concisely presented. Each volume has a general introduction to the geography and history of settlement in the region described. Distinct climate zones are defined and described within each region.

Lionel March (ed.), *The Architecture of Form*, Cambridge University Press, Cambridge, 1976. Essays by the founders of the Cambridge 'school' of architectural research, now the Martin Centre for Architectural and Urban Studies, that make the case for the use of systematic studies in investigating the determinants of architectural form. The nature and application of typology is a theme in a number of the essays.

Lionel March and Philip Steadman, *The Geometry of Environment*, RIBA, London, 1971. This pioneering study presents a wide-ranging exploration of the geometry of built form and of the value of formal models in architectural design and research. It is illustrated by a rich array of examples, many of which are directly relevant in the field of environmental design.

T. A. Markus and E. N. Morris, *Buildings, Climate and Energy*, Pitman, London, 1980. One of the standard texts on the fundamentals of building science.

Leslie Martin and Lionel March (eds), *Urban Space and Structures*, Cambridge University Press, Cambridge, 1972. The first in the series of 'Cambridge Papers on Architectural and Urban Studies'. In these essays, the emphasis is upon the urban scale. Includes the seminal studies on the relationship between court and pavilion forms of urban development.

Leslie Martin, *Buildings and Ideas: 1933–1983*, Cambridge University Press, Cambridge, 1983. The 'oeuvre complet' of Martin, who created the framework within which the Cambridge 'school' of architectural studies developed. Brings together a number of essays on architectural research and education with comprehensive descriptions of the work of his practice over more than four decades.

P. B. Medawar, *The Art of the Soluble*, Methuen, London, 1967. A collection of essays on scientific method and the nature of theory by one of the most eminent British philosophers of science.

A. Olgyay, *Solar Control and Shading Devices*, Princeton University Press, Princeton, NJ, 1977. A rigorous explanation of the principles and methods of solar shading in architecture.

Victor Olgyay, *Design with Climate: Bioclimatic Approach to Architectural Regionalism*, van Nostrand Reinhold, New York, 1963. Essential reading for all interested in environmentally responsive and responsible design. Olgyay's emphasis in the title of the book on 'Design *with* Climate' sets the work apart from almost all works on environmental design at that period, when technological determinism held sway. The book is particularly notable for the elegance of the conceptual models of 'interlocking fields of climate balance' and 'flattening the curve' in which the environmental potential of architectural form and material is clearly delineated. The case study designs for distinct climate zones of North America evince a clear climatic regionalism.

J. E. Oliver, *Climate and Man's Environment: An Introduction to Applied Climatology*, Wiley, New York, 1973. A view from the macro-scale in which the fundamentals of climate as they affect man are comprehensively and lucidly set out.

Paul Oliver (ed.), *Shelter in Africa*, Barrie & Jenkins, London, 1971. A collection of papers by a number of authors that explores the close relationship which exists between traditional architecture and indigenous cultures. The book seeks to reassert the significance of traditional architecture following the impositions of colonialism.

W. Palz (ed.). *1987 European Conference on Architecture*, H. S. Stephens & Associates, Bedford, 1987. The Commission of the European Communities has played a central role in the promotion of research and practice in the field of environmentally responsible design. The 1987 conference was the first of the sequence of such meetings that have become one of the major forums for the presentation of work from around the world.

Nikolaus Pevsner, *The Englishness of English Art*, Pelican, Harmondsworth, 1965. Pevsner's important study of the geography of art in which he sets out significant ideas relating to the question of regionalism in architecture.

R. Powell and Ken Yeang, *Rethinking the Environmental Filter*, Foreword by Kisho Kurokawa, Landmark, Singapore, 1989. The work of the Malaysian architect Ken Yeang represents one of the most cogent attempts to reconcile the imagery and technology of the modern commercial building with the agenda of the environmental movement. The book elegantly connects theory and practice and, most importantly, locates the work in the wider theoretical discourse on architectural regionalism and speculations about the future of the tropical city. Yeang has continued to develop his work and *Hamzah and Yeang: Bioclimatic Skyscrapers*, 2nd edn, Ellipsis, London, 1994, is a comprehensive survey of his designs for skyscrapers for many tropical locations.

A. Rapoport, *House Form and Culture*, Prentice-Hall, Englewood Cliffs, 1969. Rapoport's work demonstrates the relationship between climate and the form of houses in traditional architecture from around the world and shows that, from the very earliest times, buildings have transcended mere utility in acquiring value as the location of private and public ritual.

Steen E. Rasmussen, *Experiencing Architecture*, MIT Press, Cambridge, MA, 1984. The book provides one of the most approachable and perceptive accounts of the environmental experience of architecture. It is essential reading.

Richard Rogers (ed. P. Gumuchdjian), *Cities for a Small Planet*, Faber & Faber, London, 1998. A wide-ranging polemic on the future of cities, combining social and environmental concerns. Architectural examples are drawn from the work of the Richard Rogers Partnership and London is the focus of an extensive design study to illustrate the implications of the argument.

B. Rudofsky, *Architecture Without Architects: A Short Introduction to Non-Pedigreed Architecture*, Museum of Modern Art, New York, 1964; repr. University of New Mexico Press, Albuquerque, 1987. This is a key text in the documentation of vernacular building and in suggesting its significance for contemporary design.

Joseph Rykwert, *On Adam's House in Paradise: The Idea of the Primitive Hut in Architectural History*, Museum of Modern Art, New York, 1972. The idea of the primitive hut has served to illustrate the fundamental questions of the nature and purpose of architecture. These ideas have great significance for the environmental debate. Rykwert's book is the standard text on these ideas.

R. Saxon, *Atrium Buildings: Development and Design*, Architectural Press, Guildford, 1983. The emergence of the atrium form was one of the most significant developments in the design of large commercial and institutional buildings in the 1980s. This book is the most authoritative source on the subject and presents sound guidance on the underlying principles of the type. Particular attention is paid to the basis of effective environmental design. See also the author's *The Atrium Comes of Age*, Longman, London, 1994, which consolidates the substance of the earlier volume in the light of a further decade of experience.

H. A. Simon, *The Sciences of the Artificial*, MIT Press, Cambridge, MA, 1961. Simon's work was one of the first attempts to apply the methods of the natural sciences to the study of the man-made world. It had considerable influence on architectural ideology and remains thought provoking four decades later.

Philip Steadman, *The Evolution of Designs: Biological Analogy in Architecture and Applied Arts*. Cambridge University Press, Cambridge, 1979. Steadman develops a comprehensive critical review of the recurrent connection between biology and architecture and the arts. The text covers questions of formal analogy, the role of taxonomy and the idea of evolution in architectural production.

E. von Weizsacker, A. B. Lovins and L. H. Lovins, *Factor Four: Doubling Wealth, Halving Resource Use: The New Report to the Club of Rome*, Earthscan, London, 1997. A compelling polemic in which distinguished pioneers of the environmental movement present a formula for reconciling the need for continuing economic growth with the reduction of consumption of resources. A small number of architectural examples figure in the argument, a number of which have the characteristics of selective design.

S. Yannas, *Solar Energy and Housing Design*, 2 vols, Architectural Association, London, 1991. This work is one of the most comprehensive presentations of the potential of solar energy applied to the design of housing and houses in the UK. There is a discussion of general principles and an interesting selection of built projects, many of which demonstrate the difficult synthesis of combining technical innovation with architectural merit.

Appendix: Generic energy data for London and Lagos

Figures A.1–12 are energy data charts for London, UK, and Lagos, Nigeria, as described and applied in the generic design exercise in Chapter 6. The figures present data for each of the space types illustrated in Figure 6.7(a)–(d) for a range of glazing ratios.

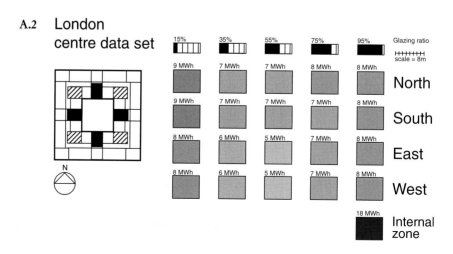

A.1 London centre data set

	15%	35%	55%	75%	95%	Glazing ratio scale = 8m
North	8 MWh	6 MWh	6 MWh	7 MWh	7 MWh	
South	8 MWh	5 MWh	6 MWh	10 MWh	11 MWh	
East	8 MWh	5 MWh	5 MWh	6 MWh	7 MWh	
West	8 MWh	5 MWh	5 MWh	6 MWh	6 MWh	
Internal zone					18 MWh	

A.2 London centre data set

	15%	35%	55%	75%	95%	Glazing ratio scale = 8m
North	9 MWh	7 MWh	7 MWh	8 MWh	8 MWh	
South	9 MWh	7 MWh	7 MWh	7 MWh	8 MWh	
East	8 MWh	6 MWh	5 MWh	7 MWh	8 MWh	
West	8 MWh	6 MWh	5 MWh	7 MWh	8 MWh	
Internal zone					18 MWh	

A.3 London
corner data set

North

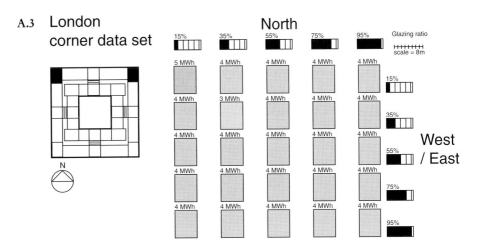

A.4 London
corner data set

South

★ air conditioning
included

discomfort: glare
or overheating

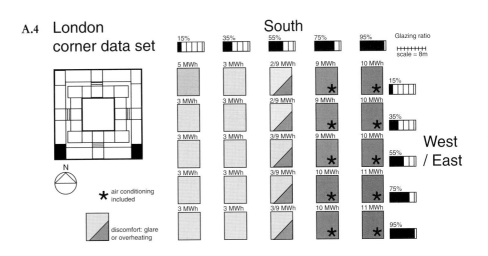

A.5 London
corner data set

South

★ air conditioning
included

discomfort: glare
or overheating

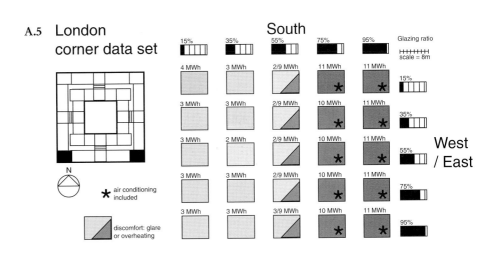

A.6 London corner data set

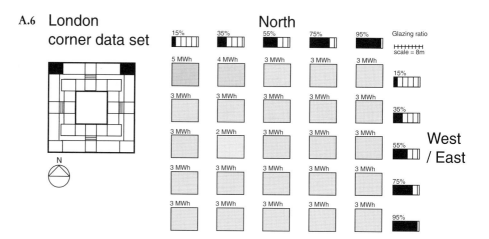

North

Glazing ratio
scale = 8m

15% 35% 55% 75% 95%

North				
5 MWh	4 MWh	3 MWh	3 MWh	3 MWh
3 MWh	3 MWh	3 MWh	3 MWh	3 MWh
3 MWh	2 MWh	3 MWh	3 MWh	3 MWh
3 MWh	3 MWh	3 MWh	3 MWh	3 MWh
3 MWh	3 MWh	3 MWh	3 MWh	3 MWh

West / East

15%
35%
55%
75%
95%

A.7 Lagos centre data set

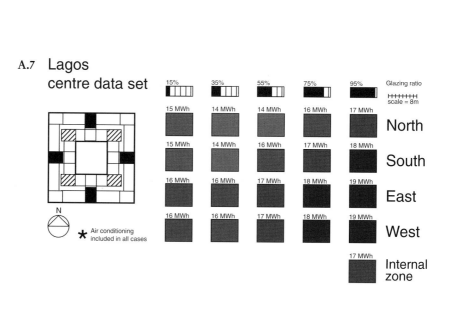

Glazing ratio
scale = 8m

15% 35% 55% 75% 95%

North				
15 MWh	14 MWh	14 MWh	16 MWh	17 MWh

South				
15 MWh	14 MWh	16 MWh	17 MWh	18 MWh

East				
16 MWh	16 MWh	17 MWh	18 MWh	19 MWh

West				
16 MWh	16 MWh	17 MWh	18 MWh	19 MWh

17 MWh Internal zone

★ Air conditioning included in all cases

A.8 Lagos centre data set

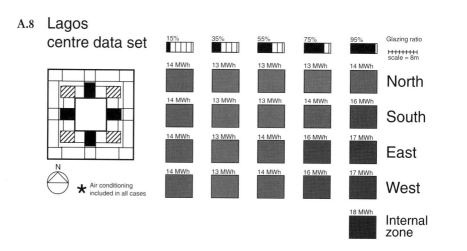

Glazing ratio
scale = 8m

15% 35% 55% 75% 95%

North				
14 MWh	13 MWh	13 MWh	13 MWh	14 MWh

South				
14 MWh	13 MWh	13 MWh	14 MWh	16 MWh

East				
14 MWh	13 MWh	14 MWh	16 MWh	17 MWh

West				
14 MWh	13 MWh	14 MWh	16 MWh	17 MWh

18 MWh Internal zone

★ Air conditioning included in all cases

A.9 Lagos
corner data set

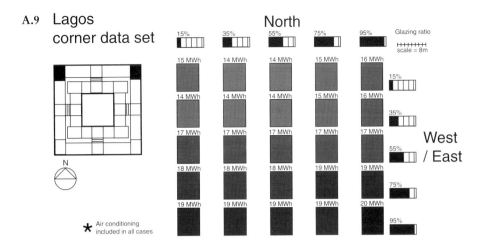

A.10 Lagos
corner data set

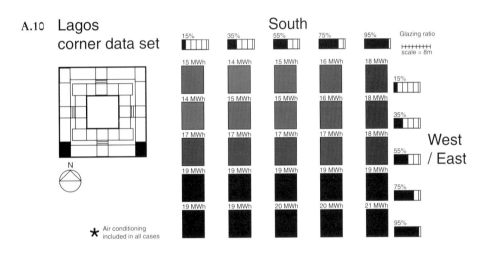

A.11 Lagos
corner data set

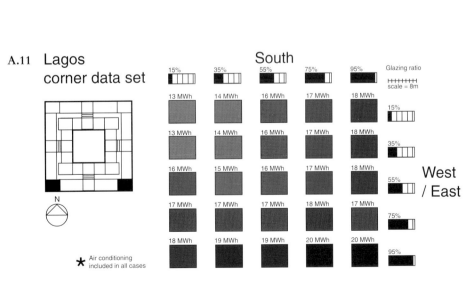

A.12 Lagos
corner data set

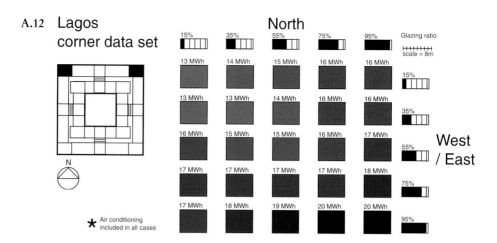

N

★ Air conditioning
included in all cases

North

West / East

Glazing ratio
scale = 8m

Index